ANCIENT DUNSTABLE

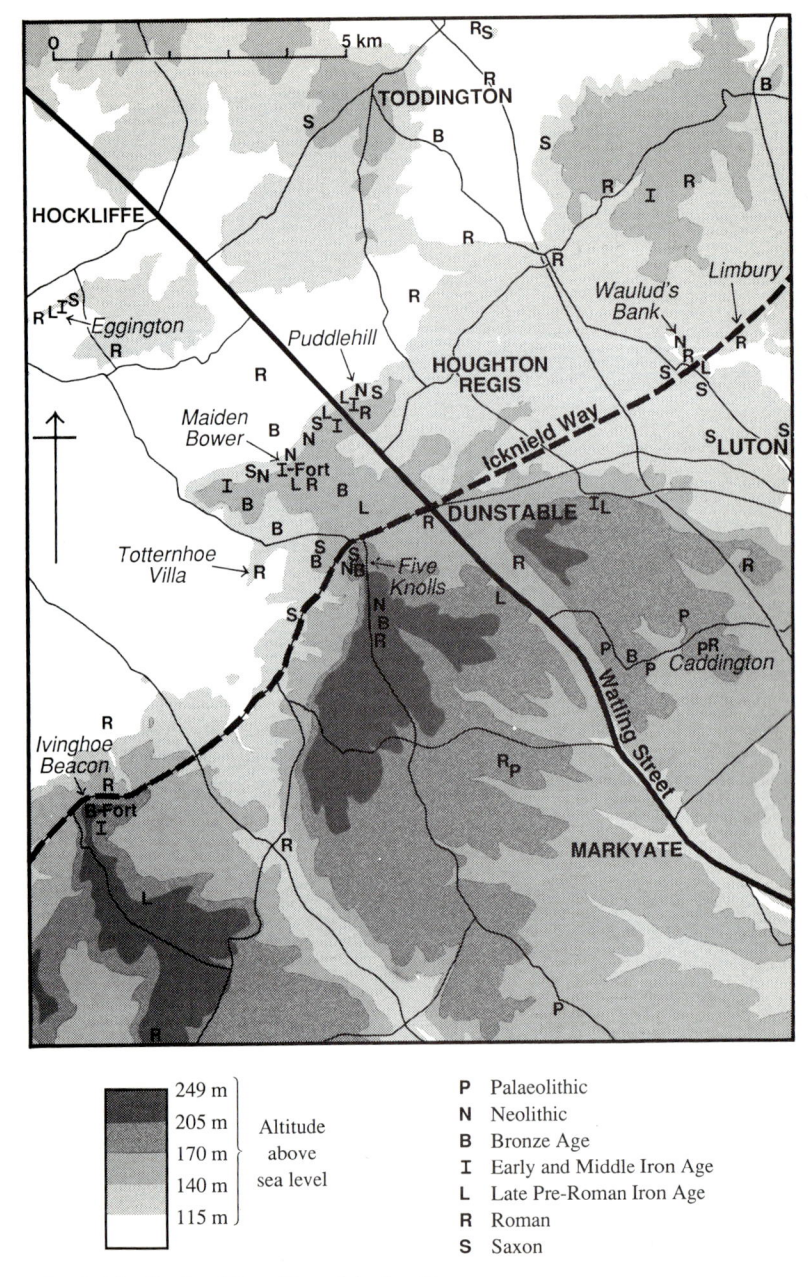

Fig. 1. Distribution Map of Local Antiquities

Ancient Dunstable

A Prehistory of the District

by
C. L. MATTHEWS

Revised and enlarged by
J. P. SCHNEIDER

Published by the
Manshead Archaeological Society of Dunstable
Bedfordshire

First published 1963
Second edition 1989

Printed by C. I. Thomas & Sons (Haverfordwest) Ltd.

ISBN 0 9515160 0 0

Foreword to First Edition

Men lived and died on the hills above Dunstable for hundreds of years before the days of written records. The district is rich in the remains of their occupation sites and their burial places – the raw material of archaeology. Their memorials lie beneath the turf and their story has to be interpreted by the excavator's trowel. This book tells their story – or as much of it as is known at present.

In 1951 a group of local people formed the Manshead Archaeological Society of Dunstable to find out as much as possible about these sites before they were irrevocably obliterated. Chalk quarrying, industrial development and new housing estates in the area all threatened to destroy the material relics of previous inhabitants. Scientific excavation had to be carried out quickly if it was to be carried out at all. Most of the sites described in these pages now no longer exist. The Society's field notes are their only record.

The original members of the Society found that their work was hampered because they did not know enough about the pattern of archaeological developments in general and about comparable sites in particular. They therefore joined the Dunstable branch of the Workers' Educational Association and applied to the Association and to the Board of Extra-Mural Studies at Cambridge for a tutor. They received tuition firstly from Miss Isobel Smith (now Dr Smith) and then from Dr John Morris, B.A., PH.D. The preparatory work for this volume has been carried out by Society members over the past ten years under the expert guidance of the latter.

The story does not end in 1963. As the final proofs of this volume were being checked, members were excavating thirty foot down a Roman well which was revealed quite unexpectedly during the demolition of a shop in High Street North. A vast amount of material remains to be excavated, studied and placed in its chronological sequence. This book is an interim report on the progress the Manshead has made in the first twelve years. It is offered to the people of Dunstable as a contribution to the heritage of the Town.

C. L. Matthews
1963

C. L. Matthews, F. S. A. (1910 – 1989)

Foreword to Second Edition

Les Matthews would have liked to produce an updated version of this book himself, but, sadly, his death earlier this year has prevented that. In the years since he wrote "Ancient Dunstable" much has been added to our knowledge of the peoples who lived in our area in past times, and this revised edition includes many sites excavated since 1963. Readers familiar with the first edition will also notice some changes in dating and interpretation. In archaeology new information constantly comes to light and new theories are developed. We have attempted here, as did Les in 1963, to give an up-to-date version of the relevant prehistory and history. In ten years' time some of today's interpretations will in their turn be out of date.

Archaeological theorists are dependent on the detailed reports written by excavators, and Les Matthews was always very aware of the duty to publish full accounts of what was found. With the help of other members of the Manshead Society and of experts in various aspects of the subject, he produced a number of reports (see Book List), all of them important contributions to British archaeology.

"Ancient Dunstable" takes into account the work of earlier and present-day archaeologists working in the district, but describes in more detail the discoveries made by the Manshead Archaeological Society of Dunstable. For interested people in the area, the Society has collected and interpreted the evidence of our past. For its members it has provided immense enjoyment in the comradeship of a shared interest. The Society was Les's creation and he was its driving force for over thirty years. This revision and republication of "Ancient Dunstable" is a team effort by members of the Society, undertaken in affectionate and grateful memory of Les.

There have been changes in the organisation of archaeology in Bedfordshire in the last twenty years: the county is no longer wholly reliant on devoted amateurs to record its threatened archaeological heritage. Bedfordshire County Council now has professional archaeologists in its Conservation Department, and the amateur role has diminished. We believe, however, that in today's specialised and expensive archaeology there is still an important place in the team for the trained amateur with detailed local knowledge, as an excavator and recorder. The value of groups willing to study and collect the evidence of the past to be found on the surface of the ground is not in dispute. Future editions of this book will, we hope, reflect the continuing enthusiasm and activity of local people, who will owe a debt, greater than they may perhaps realise, to Les Matthews.

Joan Schneider
August 1989

Contents

1 **The Old Stone Age and Middle Stone Age** 1
The Palaeolithic Period; The Mesolithic Period.

2 **The Neolithic or New Stone Age** 4
The Introduction of Farming; Causewayed Enclosures, Flint Mines and Long Barrows; Beaker Burials.

3 **The Bronze Age** 14
Bronze Age Burials; Agriculture; The Bronzesmith.

4 **The Iron Age and the Celts** 21
The Celts; The First Iron Age Farmstead on Puddlehill; Diet and Way of Life; The Pottery; The Second Farmstead; Storage Pits; Hillforts.

5 **The Middle Iron Age (c.300 B.C. – c.50 B.C.)** 42
New Settlers on Puddlehill; Enclosures, Houses and Pits; A Response to Danger; Rulers and Religion.

6 **The Late Pre-Roman Iron Age** 49
The Historical Record Begins; The Belgae; Julius Caesar: The Roman Expeditions to Britain; Tribes and Chieftains; New Settlers on Puddlehill; Cremation; Ditch Systems; The End of British Independence.

7 **The Roman Period** 59
The Effect of the Roman Conquest on Puddlehill; Roman Roads and Towns; The Boudican Revolt; The Romano-British Town of Durocobrivis; Life in Roman Dunstable; Burials; The Historical Background; Other Local Sites; The Roman Villa at Totternhoe; A Building at Bidwell.

8 **The Anglo-Saxon Settlements** 91
The Decline of the Roman Empire; The Coming of the Saxons; The Literary Evidence; The Original Settlements; The Archaeological Evidence; The Britons Retaliate: The Saxon Warrior on Puddlehill; The Saxon Conquest; Saxon Settlement on Puddlehill; Life on the Saxon Farmstead; Puddlehill Saxon Cemetery; The Saxon Cemetery at Marina Drive, Dunstable; Early Christian Cemeteries; The Mystery of the Five Knolls; A Changing Pattern.

Museums 118

Book List 119

Acknowledgments 125

Illustrations

Figures

Fig. 1	Distribution Map of Local Antiquities	Facing title page
Fig. 2	Palaeolithic Flint Tools from Caddington	2
Fig. 3	Plan of a Causewayed Enclosure	6
Fig. 4	Early Neolithic Pot from Causewayed Enclosure at Maiden Bower	7
Fig. 5	Flint Implements	8
Fig. 6	Grooved Ware – Late Neolithic Pottery from Puddlehill	9
Fig. 7	A Long Barrow	10
Fig. 8	Finds from Beaker Burial, Sewell	12
Fig. 9	Types of Early Bronze Age Barrow	15
Fig. 10	Bronze Dagger from Cremation at Marina Drive	16
Fig. 11	Bronze Pin from Late Bronze Age Settlement, Totternhoe	16
Fig. 12	Collared Urn from Barrow 5, Five Knolls	18
Fig. 13	Late Bronze Age Pottery	19
Fig. 14	Bronze Sword Blade found at Totternhoe	20
Fig. 15	Plan of Iron Age Features on Puddlehill	22
Fig. 16	First Iron Age House on Puddlehill	24
Fig. 17	Pottery from First Iron Age Farmstead	26
Fig. 18	Second Iron Age House on Puddlehill	28
Fig. 19	Pottery from the Second Iron Age Farmstead	30
Fig. 20	Sections through two Storage Pits	33
Fig. 21	Maiden Bower – Sections through Rampart and Ditch	37
Fig. 22	Maiden Bower – Section through Silted-up Ditch	38
Fig. 23	Pottery of the Middle Iron Age Period, Puddlehill	42
Fig. 24	Finds from the Middle Iron Age Farmstead, Puddlehill	46
Fig. 25	Pot from Enclosure III, showing Influence of Late Iron Age style	47
Fig. 26	Bronze Mirror found at Old Warden	52
Fig. 27	Pottery of the Late Pre-Roman Iron Age, Puddlehill	53
Fig. 28	Bronze Objects of the Late Iron Age, Puddlehill	55
Fig. 29	Coin of Cunobelinus (10–40 A.D.) found in Leagrave	56
Fig. 30	Bronze Brooch from Puddlehill	63
Fig. 31	Pottery from Roman Dunstable	64
Fig. 32	Plan of Dunstable showing Roman Find Spots	66
Fig. 33	A Roman-style Tiled Roof	68
Fig. 34	Finds from a Roman well in Dunstable	69
Fig. 35	Section through Cemetery Ditch and Grave	73
Fig. 36	Two Burials in the Dunstable Romano-British Cemetery	75

Fig. 37 Pottery and Glass found with Burials	78
Fig. 38 Jewellery found in a Little Girl's Grave	79
Fig. 39 Plan of Roman Villa at Totternhoe	83
Fig. 40 Pottery from the Totternhoe Villa	86
Fig. 41 Early Saxon Brooches from Cemetery in Luton	96
Fig. 42 Cremation Urn from Argyll Avenue	97
Fig. 43 Plan of Saxon Sites North of Dunstable	100
Fig. 44 Late Sixth Century Pots	101
Fig. 45 Seventh Century Pottery from Farmstead on Puddlehill	102
Fig. 46 Saxon Building 4 from Puddlehill	103
Fig. 47 Saxon Building 6 from Puddlehill	105
Fig. 48 Comb and Spindle Whorl, Puddlehill	106
Fig. 49 Saucer Brooch buried at Puddlehill	109
Fig. 50 Plan of Marina Drive Cemetery	110
Fig. 51 Grave Goods from Marina Drive Cemetery	111
Fig. 52 Grave Goods from Marina Drive Cemetery	112

Plates

Plate 1 Fragments of Beaker from Sewell	13
Plate 2 Reconstruction of an Iron Age House	25
Plate 3 Carinated Bowls from Second Iron Age Farmstead	31
Plate 4 Skeleton in Storage Pit	34
Plate 5 Aerial Photograph of Maiden Bower	36
Plate 6 Maiden Bower – Postholes in Fill of Ditch	39
Plate 7 Decorated Pot Lid	43
Plate 8 Carbonised Bread Roll	44
Plate 9 A Roman Corn Drying Kiln, Puddlehill	60
Plate 10 Silver Ring from Roman Well	70
Plate 11 Skull of Barbary Ape from Roman Cesspit	71
Plate 12 Mutilated Skeleton	76
Plate 13 Decapitated Skeleton	77
Plate 14 Skeletons in Top of Well	80
Plate 15 Totternhoe Roman Villa Hypocaust	84
Plate 16 Part of Mosaic Floor, Totternhoe Roman Villa	87
Plate 17 Tessellated Floor covered by Cobbling, Totternhoe Villa	88
Plate 18 Wooden Piles, Bidwell	89
Plate 19 Saxon Warrior, Puddlehill	98
Plate 20 Saxon Building 5, Puddlehill	104
Plate 21 Jewellery from Burial at Puddlehill	108

CHAPTER 1

The Old Stone Age and Middle Stone Age
(Palaeolithic and Mesolithic)

The Palaeolithic Period

The prehistory of Dunstable and its neighbourhood begins long before the rolling downland, the escarpments and fertile valleys that make up today's landscape had been formed. It starts with the period known to archaeologists as the Palaeolithic or Old Stone Age, which, in the light of present knowledge dates to somewhere over two million years ago and lasted until the ending of the last Ice Age about 8,000 B.C.

During this immense period of time, this country and the whole of northern Europe underwent many climatic changes that varied between arctic cold and tropical heat. The action of glaciers during the cold periods, the rushing waters of great rivers as the ice melted and retreated, and the strong winds that tore across the barren countryside that the ice caps left behind, all helped to wash and grind away the beds of upper chalk laid down some seventy million years ago. It was this weathering action which formed pockets of gravel, carved out the valleys and left great river beds which form the gaps in the Chiltern Hills. A valley typical of the glacial action, steep-sided and flat-bottomed, can be seen at the foot of Ivinghoe Beacon. It is known locally as Coombe Hole. One of the ancient river beds now forms the gap in the hills between Blows and Dunstable Downs – the gap chosen by the Romans for their great military road, the Watling Street. The laying of drains in this valley during the building of the Downside Estate revealed water-deposited gravels and rolled pebbles more than 6 m deep and excavations dug into the valley sides showed swirls of pebbles where the great river of the past had forced its way through the hills and spread over the surrounding countryside.

During the Ice Ages many wild animals such as woolly rhinoceros, mammoth, arctic fox and reindeer roamed the countryside and gradually retreated northwards as the ice sheet melted and the climate became warmer, to be followed during the semi-tropical climate by elephant, lion, hippopotamus, bear and hyena. Discoveries of the bones of these animals have been made in many parts of Britain.

At this time Britain was still joined to the Continent and during warmer periods, when the ice retreated northwards, races of early human-like creatures were able to spread into our land, following the wild animals which they hunted for food. The remains of these, together with flint implements, are often found in gravel pits. South Bedfordshire, and particularly the Dunstable area, is comparatively rich in these finds. The hilltops to the south of Dunstable are capped with a deposit of clay that used to be worked for

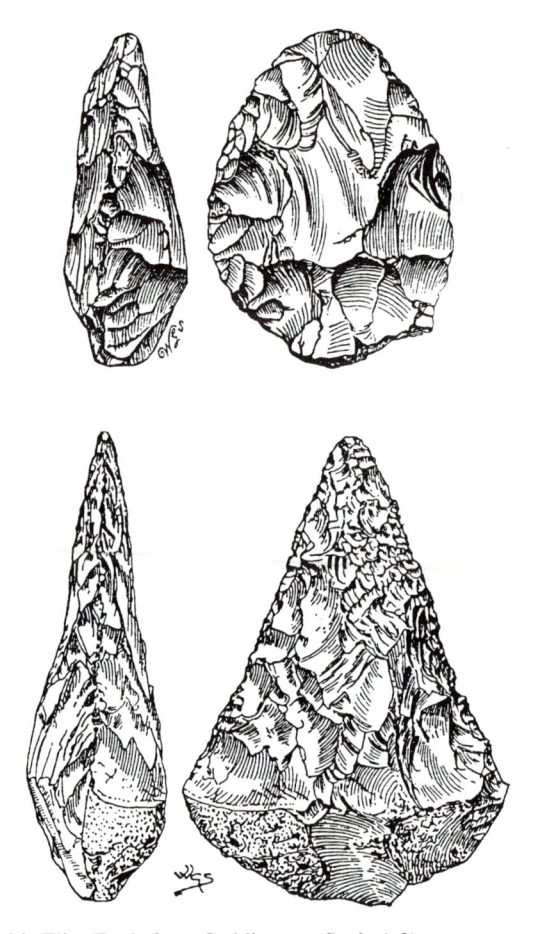

Fig. 2. Palaeolithic Flint Tools from Caddington (Scale 1:2).
Drawn by Worthington G. Smith.

brick-making. The late Worthington G. Smith of Dunstable studied the faces of these clay pits and discovered levels containing flint implements. He found that a pre-glacial land surface appeared in the pits at Round Green, Caddington, Kensworth, Whipsnade and Gaddesden Row. Some fine examples of implements and tools found by him can be seen in Luton Museum and in the British Museum.

At Caddington he discovered an actual living and working place of the Lower Palaeolithic period, where early people had made tools and weapons:

stone implements were found both in both rough and highly finished states, together with hundreds of flint chips or flakes. Worthington Smith knew that these flakes were lying just where they had fallen as the stone-age worker sat chipping out tools, because the edges of the flakes were still sharp enough to cut the fingers, and many of the pieces could be fitted exactly together to re-create the nodule of flint from which they had been struck.

There were in fact separate stone age working areas at Caddington, producing flint tools with different techniques, known as "Acheulian" and "Levalloisian" after the places in France where such flints were first identified. This suggests that the same small area was occupied at quite different periods, perhaps separated by thousands of years, and all more than 100,000 years ago. These working floors were buried by a glacial drift that varied from three to twelve metres deep.

During the last inter-glacial period the primitive hominids of the Lower and Middle Palaeolithic periods, such as those at Caddington, were succeeded by the ancestors of the modern human race. These Upper Palaeolithic peoples are best known by their skilful paintings in the limestone caves of France and Spain.

The Mesolithic Period

When the ice retreated from Britain for the last time, about 10,000 years ago, the climate gradually changed over many centuries, and the contours of the countryside that we know today took shape. The people who returned again to Britain have been called the Mesolithic (Middle Stone Age) people. Bedfordshire was covered by forest, bush and marsh. The Dunstable Downs were covered by scrub and the valleys of Totternhoe, Eaton Bray and Tilsworth were swamps. It was during this period that Britain was cut off from the continent. The approximate date at which our land became an island is given as 6,000 B.C.

Few traces of Mesolithic people have as yet been found in Bedfordshire. They lived by hunting and fishing and their culture is represented by small, geometrically-shaped flint implements that were inserted into bone and wooden shafts for fish spears and arrows. Long blades were used as knives. The bow and arrow was the chief hunting weapon.

The nearest recorded Mesolithic sites to Dunstable are on the chalk at Blows Downs and Waulud's Bank, and on the sand and gravels at Eggington and Leighton Buzzard.

These sites were occupied when farming first began in Britain. Agriculture was introduced from the Continent around 3,500 B.C. and this was the start of the period of prehistory known as the Neolithic or New Stone Age.

CHAPTER 2

The Neolithic or New Stone Age Period

The Introduction of Farming

During the Mesolithic era in Britain, a new way of life had evolved on the flood plains of the Nile and in the valleys of the Tigris and Euphrates. People had learned to domesticate animals and to cultivate crops. Having mastered these arts, people were no longer dependent upon a food gathering economy, and were able to grow more than their needs. This in time led to an increase in population and the ability to live in static communities with a wider exchange of ideas.

From these twin centres of agricultural origins and material development the new economy spread across Europe and had arrived in Britain by 3,500 B.C.

The types of corn they cultivated and some of the animals which were domesticated were not native to this country, so they must have been imported from the Continent, but whether they were accompanied into Britain by a large number of immigrants is unknown. No close resemblance between the ways of life at that time on the two sides of the Channel and the North Sea has been found, so it is possible that the Mesolithic population in Britain acquired the animals and cereals from the Continent for themselves.

Another important innovation at this period was the manufacture of pottery to make containers. Previously these had been of wood, basketwork or leather. Almost any clay can be used to make pottery: it is mixed with water till it is smooth and workable, moulded into shape, allowed to dry until "leather hard" and then baked in a fire. In Britain, before the late first century B.C., firing was done in an ordinary hearth or a bonfire and not in a purpose-built kiln. The heat was only sufficient to produce a rather porous fabric. From earliest times potters mixed other substances with the clay, such as sand, crushed stone or crushed shell (fresh or fossilised). This process is called "filling" or "tempering" the clay. It reduces shrinkage during the drying stage and makes the pot less likely to crack while being fired.

Potters at different times and places had different preferences for "fillers" and this, as well as changing fashions in shape and decoration, helps archaeologists to identify the pots they find. Because pottery does not decay like wood or other organic materials, it is very important on archaeological sites, and the broken pieces, called "sherds", form a large proportion of finds from the Neolithic period onwards.

The technique must have been learned from continental potters, although there is no close similarity between the earliest known British pots and those of the same period found abroad. It seems that the native Mesolithic peoples absorbed the new skills of agriculture and manufacture, along with any immigrants who brought them over, and the way of life developed here along its own, insular path.

Farming enabled a surplus of food to be produced. No longer did the inhabitants need to hunt and fish all the year round, or follow migrating herds of wild animals. They could settle down, and they had spare time and manpower to co-operate in large construction projects.

Causewayed Enclosures, Flint Mines and Long Barrows

These people were responsible for the earliest types of monument on the face of our countryside: causewayed enclosures; flint mines; and burial mounds, called "long barrows".

They were the first people to till the land around Dunstable, and evidence that they settled here is provided by the causewayed enclosure beneath the later Iron Age fort at Maiden Bower. During chalk digging in the 1890s Worthington Smith recorded a series of ditches containing animal bones, flints and Neolithic pottery, although he did not at the time understand the significance of the site. We now believe that these ditches were part of a Neolithic causewayed enclosure, so called from the way the site was laid out (Fig. 3). An area of ground was surrounded by one or more rings made up of short lengths of ditch. "Causeways" were left between the ends of the ditches, and the earth that had been dug out was piled into banks, which, like the ditches, were not continuous.

The purpose of these enclosures is not entirely understood. They were not fortifications. It is thought that they may have acted as centres serving a wide area for the practice of initiation ceremonies, weddings, trade, exchange, and harvest celebrations: a combination of cathedral, market place and fair ground.

Any banks of the Neolithic enclosure at Maiden Bower have long since disappeared, but some of the ditches can be seen today on the quarry edge that just cuts into the Iron Age earthwork we call Maiden Bower, built on the same site more than two thousand years later.

The dating of this site to the early Neolithic period is established by the many finds, which include antler picks, probably used to dig the ditches, a comb made from deer antler, and pottery. The pots of this period normally have rounded bases and are either plain or have simple decoration (Fig. 4).

Flint implements are frequently found (Fig. 5) and Worthington Smith picked up hundreds within Maiden Bower and the surrounding fields. Polished flint axes, a feature of this culture, are also found in the Dunstable area. Fig. 5 shows broken ones found at Studham and in the ring ditch on Brewers Hill (Chapter 3). The flint used for the larger tools was usually mined. The reason for this is that flint nodules found lying on the ground surface have been exposed to the elements, and usually contain flaws, and so the Neolithic people preferred to dig for the flint and acquire it from the original strata in the chalk. No flint mines have been found in this area, but hollows on the tops of hills nearby, on Pitstone Hill for example, may well be the scars of Neolithic flint mines. The large number of fossil sea urchins placed with a prehistoric burial on Dunstable Downs recorded by Worthington Smith show that someone had excavated deep into the chalk where these fossils are found, perhaps looking for flint. The largest area of Neolithic flint mines to be seen today is at Grimes Graves near Weeting in Norfolk. These cover thirty-four acres. Such extensive mining indicates a flint factory, and is the first evidence in Britain of people engaging in a specialised trade for a living. It is thought that these flint miners produced

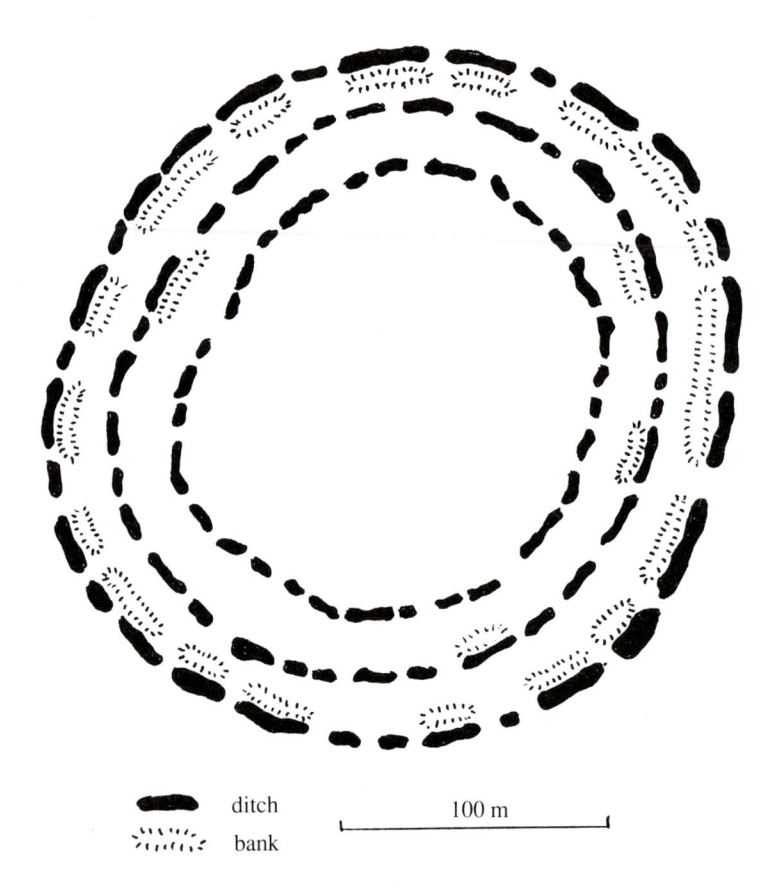

Fig. 3. Plan of a Causewayed Enclosure.

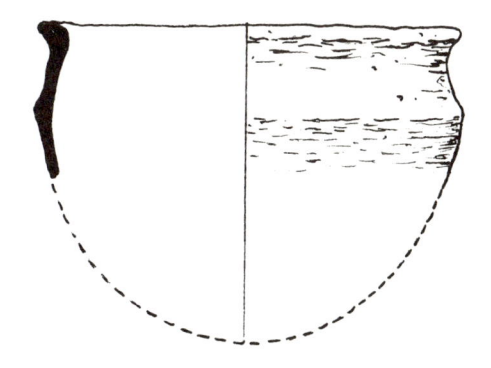

Fig. 4. Early Neolithic pot from Causewayed Enclosure ditch at Maiden Bower (Scale 1:4). Only the upper part was found, but we can guess the shape of the base (dotted line) from similar pots.

rough axe blanks for export, to be polished by the recipient. The most suitable trade route would be along what is today the Icknield Way, a routeway which originated in prehistoric times and which follows the northern edge of the sand and chalk ridges, including the Chiltern Hills, from the Norfolk Edge down to Salisbury Plain.

Flint mines in Sussex started in the early part of the Neolithic, but the hey-day of activity at Grimes Graves seems to have been later, roughly 2,500 to 1,800 B.C., and pottery of this later time, called "Grooved Ware", has also been found near Dunstable. These pots are flat-bottomed and lavishly decorated with grooves, ridges and stab marks. One pot (Fig. 6 c), a wide dish with a chequered pattern on the inside, is very similar to one found at Grimes Graves.

The local finds of Grooved Ware come from eight small pits on Puddlehill, north of Houghton Regis. Houses and settlements of the Neolithic period are very rarely found in Britain. Usually the only evidence of where the people lived is the flint implements found in ploughed fields, or the material from such pits filled with rubbish. Perhaps they were originally dug to store grain (as was done later, in the Iron Age) but when we find them they have been used as dustbins by the people living nearby. The pits on Puddlehill contained wood ash, bones from pigs, sheep and cattle (including wild aurochs), broken pottery, chips of flint and charred hazel nut shells. We can picture the people sitting round their fire cracking nuts and throwing the shells in the embers. Later on they swept up the rubbish and put it in the pit.

The large proportion of pork bones in the pits suggests there were tracts of

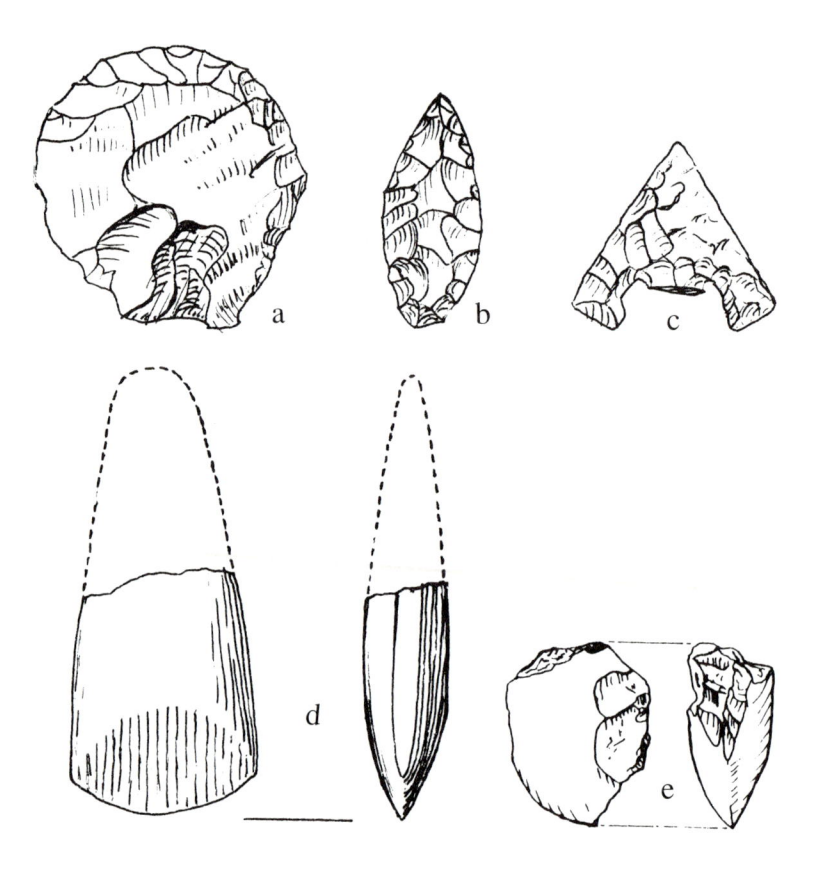

Fig. 5. Flint implements (*a, b, c* actual size, *d, e* half size). *a,* scraper; *b,* Neolithic leaf-shaped arrow head; *c,* Bronze Age barbed-and-tanged arrow head (tang broken); *d* and *e,* polished stone axes, broken. *d,* from Studham; *e,* from Brewers Hill ring ditch.

woodland, where pigs and cattle, wild or domesticated, could have lived, as well as grassland for the sheep.

One way in which the early Neolithic people of south-east Britain disposed of their dead was by burial in communal graves. These were built of timber and turf, and covered by a large mound of earth or chalk. They are called "Long Barrows" ("barrow" is a term used for an ancient burial mound) and can be seen on the chalk downs of southern England as long, grass-covered mounds (Fig. 7). A mound that stood in Union Street in

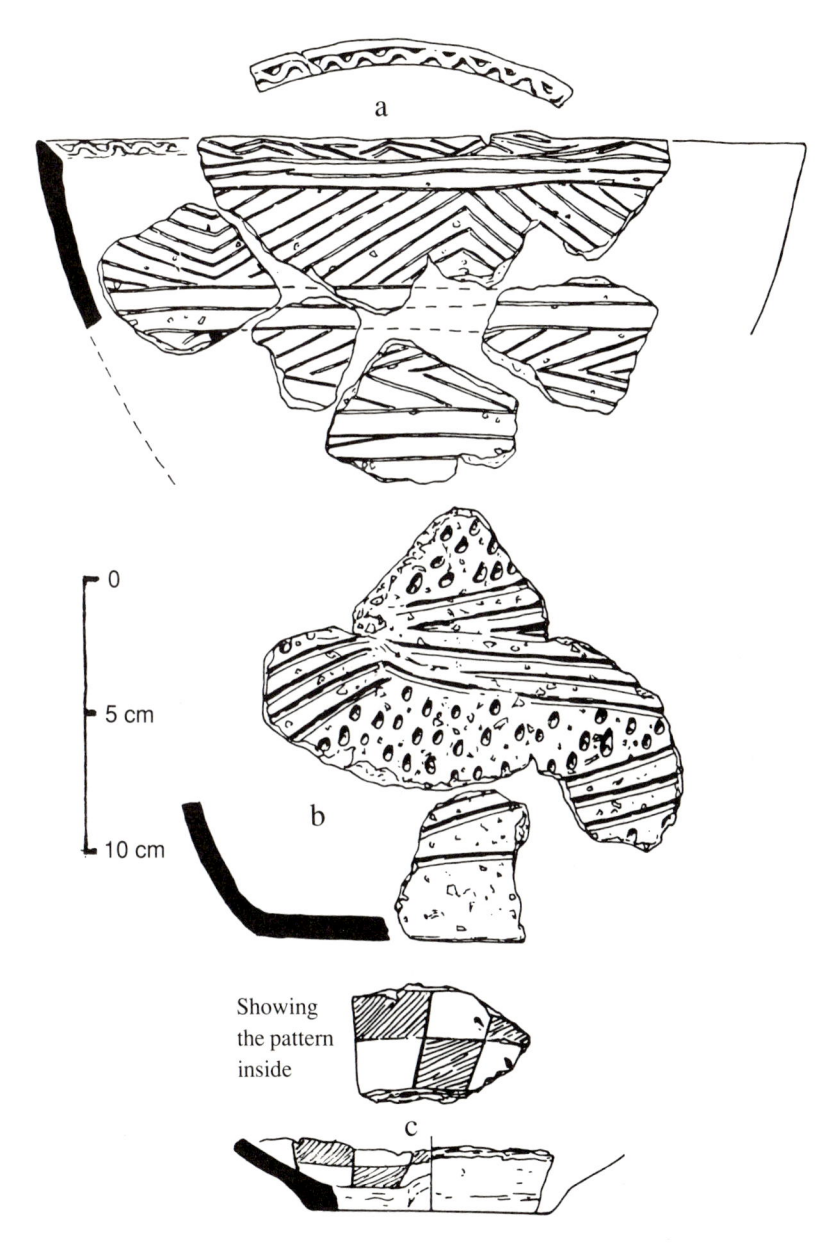

Fig. 6. Grooved Ware – late Neolithic pottery from Puddlehill.

Dunstable was considered by some to have been such a burial place, but the writer (C.L.M.) saw a surviving remnant of this destroyed, and it was in fact a natural mound of virgin chalk. There stands on Dunstable Downs a long, low mound, as yet unexcavated, that may be one of the sepulchres of these Neolithic people, but it is more probably an artificial rabbit warren of Medieval date.

By the late Neolithic period causewayed enclosures were no longer being constructed, but a new type of earthwork appeared in our countryside: a circular ditch with a bank either inside or outside it and with one or more entrances. Archaeologists believe these were religious centres, and call them "henges", after Stonehenge, the best known example. None of these has been certainly identified near Dunstable, but it is possible that the earthwork Waulud's Bank at Leagrave is in fact a henge.

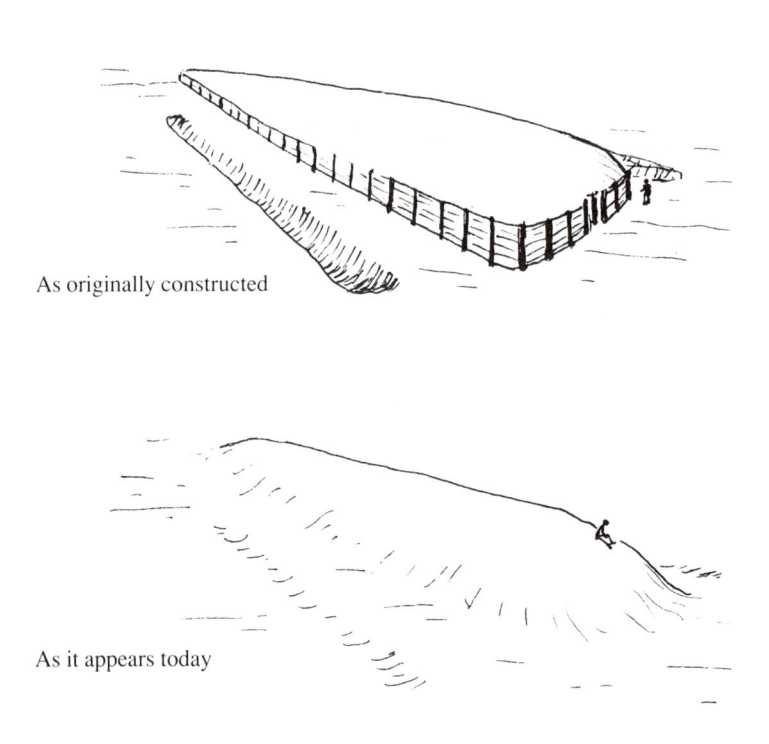

As originally constructed

As it appears today

Fig. 7. A Long Barrow

Beaker Burials

A new style of pot appeared alongside the Grooved Ware and other late Neolithic styles. This was the beaker, a well-made, distinctively-decorated drinking vessel, also known over a wide area of the rest of Europe. The beakers are usually found with burials of individuals under circular mounds (or "barrows") surrounded by a ditch. The dead person was buried lying in a hunched-up position, knees up to the chest, and this is called a "crouched burial". As well as the beaker, often flint arrow heads and other archer's gear and even personal treasures of copper, bronze or gold, are found with the skeleton.

Not far to the west of Maiden Bower a crouched burial with a beaker and other objects was found. A second burial, partly over the first, seems to have been added later, perhaps into a mound which once covered the grave but which has disappeared in the 4,000 years that have since gone by.

This beaker burial at Sewell is particularly important, as it contained, besides an archer's polished stone wrist-guard and a bone toggle, a spiral-headed pin made of bronze (Fig. 8). Metal-working had not been known in Britain before this period, and this pin is one of the earliest objects of bronze to be found in this country. It may have been an import from the Rhine Valley in Germany. Because of the importance of this burial, discovered during quarrying and excavated by the Manshead Society, the finds were donated to the British Museum, where they are on display.

Archaeologists used to believe that the Beaker pottery, the new fashion in burial and the knowledge of metal-working were brought to Britain by invaders or immigrants who were given the name of the "Beaker People". Now they are less sure, and some suggest that the new pottery and metalwork were acquired by trade, as prestige objects, as we might buy jewellery of diamonds and gold, and that the custom of individual burial under a round barrow was the popularisation of a funeral rite that we know had sometimes been practised here much earlier in the Neolithic period.

In the late Neolithic period several separate traditions of pottery-making seem to have co-existed without mixing: for instance Beakers, Grooved Ware, and Peterborough Ware. And although all potsherds from the Puddlehill pits belong to the Grooved Ware style, they represent three separate sub-divisions of that style.

Whether or not "Beaker People" were a group of immigrants to this country, their burial mounds seem to have been regarded with respect, and barrows often had other burials inserted into them at a later date.

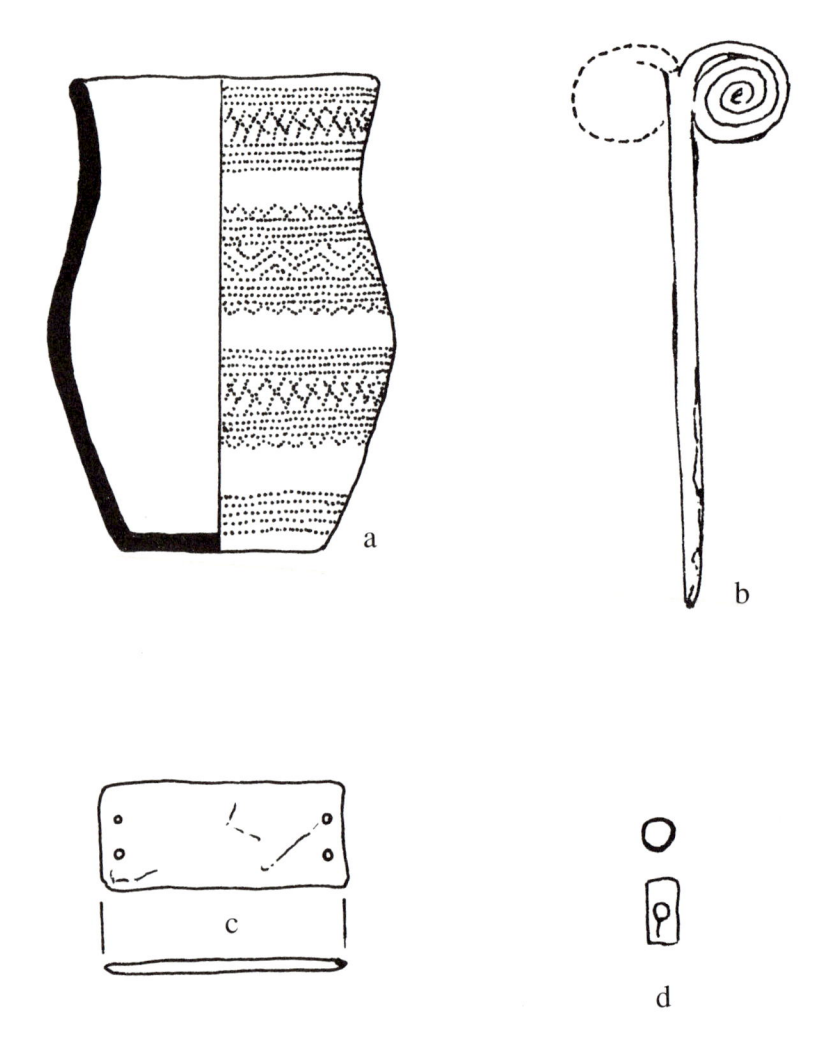

Fig. 8. Finds from the Beaker Burial, Sewell.
a   Beaker (Scale 1:3)
b   Bronze Pin (Actual size)
c   Polished Stone Wrist-guard (Scale 1:3)
d   Bone Toggle (Scale 1:3)

Plate 1. Fragments of beaker from Sewell.

CHAPTER 3

The Bronze Age

It is thought that bronze came into use in Britain just before 2,000 B.C. and the metal has given its name to the archaeological period.

Bronze Age Burials

Circular barrows of various kinds were constructed as burial mounds in the early Bronze Age, and the Five Knolls on Dunstable Downs form a cemetery of this period. Within this group of barrows there are various types (Fig. 9). Probably the earliest is a simple circular mound, with or without a ditch around it, intended for the burial of a single body. This type is known as a "bowl barrow". There are two bowl barrows in the Five Knolls group. Worthington Smith recorded two others on the Downs, one near the Golf House, and the other near the Whipsnade turn on the highest point of the Downs. In the first of these a young woman and her child had been buried together, surrounded by fossil sea urchins dug from the chalk nearby.

The other three of the Five Knolls are known as "bell barrows". These are recognised by a shelf of ground, called a "berm", of varying width separating the mound from an encircling ditch. One of these monuments was excavated during the late 1920s and the primary burial can be seen in Luton Museum. This is a woman who had been buried in a crouched position with the knees strapped under the chin. This was the usual position of burial. The Society has found skeletons lying in small pits in this crouched position near Totternhoe Knolls and on the hill at Pitstone. Worthington Smith reported them at Sewell, and undoubtedly many more existed on the chalk hills surrounding Dunstable, but have been destroyed by ploughing.

Another type of barrow belonging to the period is the "pond barrow". Two of these can also be seen on Dunstable Downs adjoining the Five Knolls bell barrows on the eastern side. They are shallow depressions surrounded by an embanked rim.

Practically all that is known about the Bronze Age peoples, particularly those of the early Bronze Age, comes from their burial rites and the religious temples they have left us. The great circles of sarsen stones at Stonehenge and Avebury were in use during the Bronze Age, although the earthworks originated in the Neolithic period. They are monuments of such size that they surely indicate that this plain in Wiltshire was the centre of a religious unity that covered most of Britain. Many Bronze Age people travelling along the Icknield Way through the Dunstable area, perhaps halting awhile at the local shrine of Waulud's Bank, must have been familiar with these great religious monuments of Wessex. Stonehenge is a temple unique in Europe.

As the Bronze Age developed, burial rites changed and for the next

Bowl Barrow

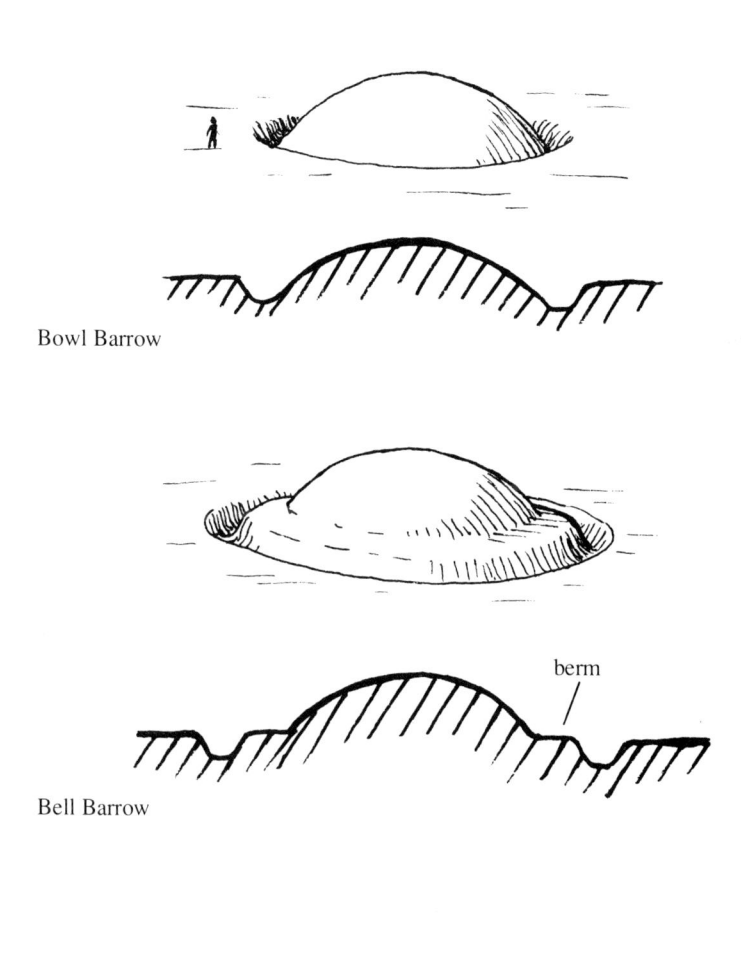

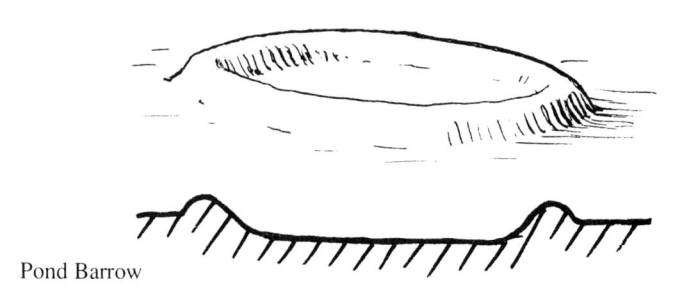

Bell Barrow

berm

Pond Barrow

Fig. 9. Types of Early Bronze Age Barrow

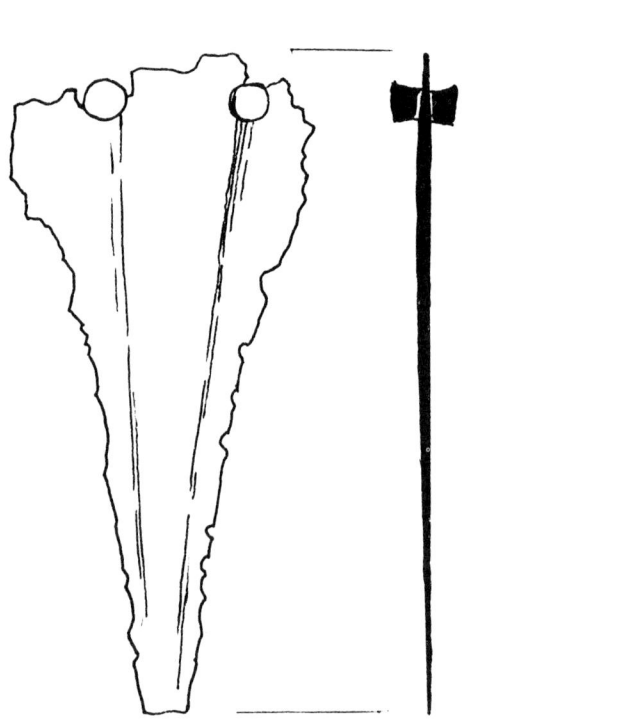

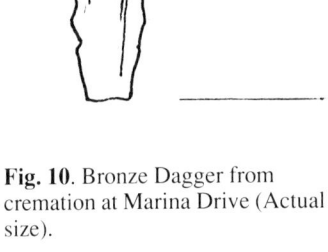

Fig. 10. Bronze Dagger from cremation at Marina Drive (Actual size).

Fig. 11. Bronze Pin from Late Bronze Age Settlement, Totternhoe (Actual size).

thousand years or so it was the practice to cremate the dead. Sometimes the burnt bones were collected and placed into urns and buried in the mounds over earlier interments. Several of these "secondary" burial urns have been recorded from the Five Knolls on Dunstable Downs. Sometimes the bones were collected into perishable containers such as a skin bag or woven basket and placed in a small pit. The area was then surrounded by a ditch, and the excavated chalk piled above the burial. The Society discovered such a burial when they were excavating the Anglo-Saxon cemetery at Marina Drive (Chapter 8). The cremated bones had been collected and placed in a small pit together with a bronze dagger belonging to the dead man. This simple dagger can be dated to between 2,000 and 1,500 B.C. When the bones had been put into the pit a circle was scribed around the area and a ditch 3 m wide and 1 m deep was dug to mark the "hallowed" place. The excavated chalk was heaped over the burial. No fewer than five such burial places have been excavated by the Society on the Totternhoe Ridge during the chalk working by the Rugby Portland Cement Company, and another before houses were built near Brewers Hill.

All surface traces of the mounds that once covered these burials have been ploughed away, but occasionally the ditches can be seen from the air as circular marks in growing crops. There is a large ring ditch of this kind near Houghton Way at Totternhoe, and yet another in the fields at Sewell. These vary in size: two excavated by the Society at Totternhoe measured about 18 m and 23 m across; another, which contained a cremation urn, was only 7 m across with a correspondingly shallower ditch.

Although we know how and where these people – or at least the important chiefs – were buried, we do not know where they lived. Their domestic pottery or camp sites are rarely found. It is only by studying the changing styles in pottery used as cinerary urns and the development of their bronze weapons and implements that the people can be placed into a chronological time sequence.

The intricacy of pottery development and change is a matter for the expert. The cinerary urn found in Barrow No. 5 on Dunstable Downs (Fig. 12), is of a type called a "collared urn", of the middle Bronze Age. During the late Bronze Age the collar survived as an applied moulding around the body of a pot known as a "bucket urn" (Fig. 13). Bucket urns containing cremations are usually found in some numbers buried in close proximity to each other. Urn fields have been found at Elstow, Kempston and Toddington in Bedfordshire, but they are only found by chance since no surface evidence of their location exists.

Agriculture

The population increased during the Bronze Age and marginal land was brought into cultivation. The terraces or lynchets that form steps along the sides of our Downs were created at times when every bit of land was needed for food growing. By ploughing or digging the ground along the hillside, the soil eroded from the higher land to the lower. The upper denuded side is known as the negative lynchet; the lower as the positive. Some of these lynchets may have been formed in the Bronze Age, whilst others are believed to be Medieval in date.

The writer (C.L.M.) found the site of a late Bronze Age village or settlement at Totternhoe many years ago. The site was partially excavated by the Dunstable Rover Scouts, and the large bucket-like pots together with a mass of carbonised wheat can be seen in Luton Museum. The wheat is a primitive form of bread wheat probably grown during the late Bronze Age on the lynchets that border the Totternhoe Ridge.

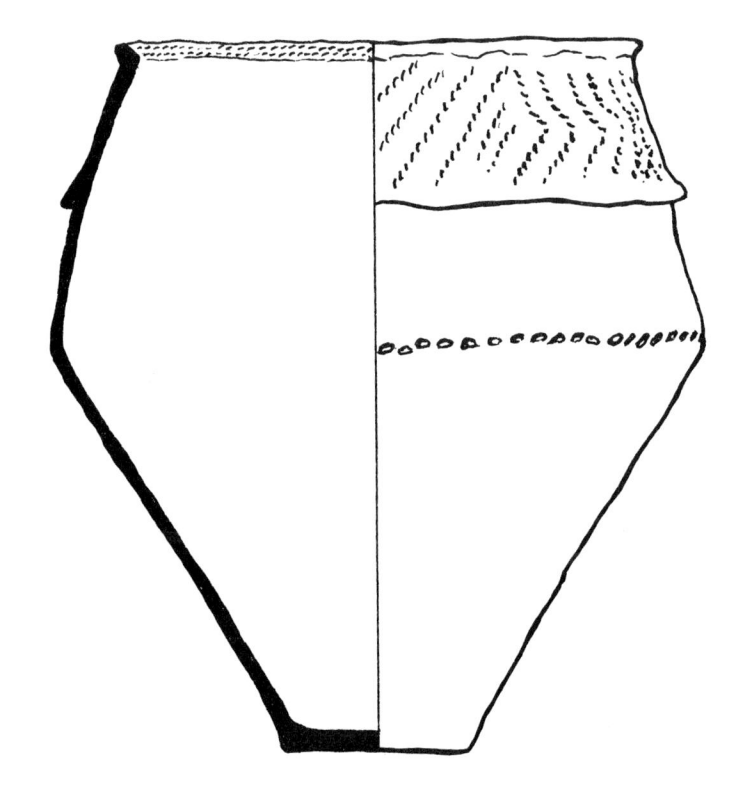

Fig. 12. Collared Urn from Barrow 5, Five Knolls (Scale 1:4). A cinerary urn (that is one used for a cremation). Archaeological drawings show the thickness of the pot and any interior decoration on the left. On the right the outside decoration is drawn.

The Bronzesmith

At the beginning of the Bronze Age, metal weapons were probably the possession of the wealthy, or tribal chieftains. Ordinary people used flint which was still worked with great skill. Barbed and tanged flint arrowheads are frequently found (Fig. 5 *c*) and, less frequently, highly polished mace heads.

During the middle Bronze Age, bronze tools came into much wider use. They were probably purchased from travelling bronzesmiths who had a "corner" in the marketing of bronze, probably obtained from Cornwall.

Our knowledge of the tools and weapons of the later Bronze Age comes largely from "hoards"; that is, deposits of bronze articles found buried together. These often include broken items and scrap metal, and it is believed they belonged to bronze-workers, who would take old items from their customers in part-exchange for new. Sometimes these were deposited for safety, to be used later, but were never collected.

"Hoards" of a different kind are sometimes recovered from rivers, springs or bogs. The climate, which had been warm and dry in the early Bronze Age, became cooler and wetter after about 1,000 B.C. and the way of life changed. The old religious sites concerned with sun worship, like Stonehenge, were abandoned, and barrows were no longer erected. A new cult of water gods and goddesses would explain the depositing of bronze objects as "votive" offerings in streams and other wet places.

A farmer in Tilsworth remembers finding a bronze spear-head while

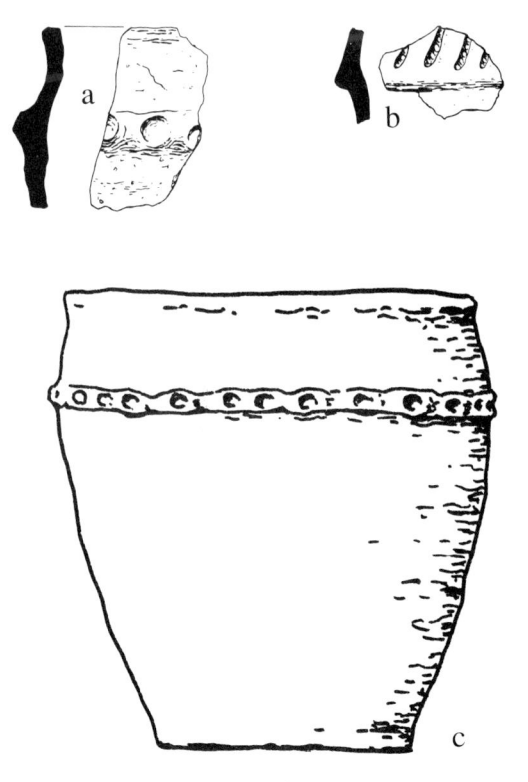

Fig. 13. Late Bronze Age Pottery. *a* and *b*, Fragments of a Bucket Urn and a Collared Urn from Totternhoe Bronzesmith's site (Scale 1:2); *c*, A Bucket Urn (Scale 1:4).

ploughing a field where silt had been dredged from a brook, and a sword-blade was discovered in an outhouse near a spring in Totternhoe, where it was being used to chop wood (Fig. 14).

A bronzesmith may have camped just two kilometres to the north-west of Dunstable. The Society found a circle of postholes showing where his hut had stood, and nearby a small pit dug into the chalk that had been subjected to great heat. The chalk of the pit had been burnt to a depth of 12 cm. This could only have been caused by forced heat such as that produced by bellows. Near the hut and forge was a series of postholes in pairs and groups of three set in a triangle. These were perhaps drying racks for the hides he received in payment for his smithing. This site was identified by the broken pottery that had been left scattered around the hut, including part of a collared urn decorated with cord impressions and pots with applied bands (Fig. 13): the bucket urns of the late Bronze Age.

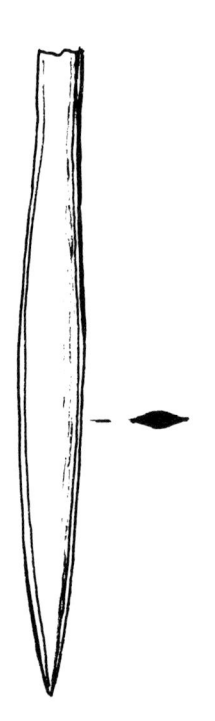

A sign that this was a period of stress, with competition for farmland when the wetter climate reclaimed hills as moorland and valleys as marsh, is the construction of the first "hillforts". On Ivinghoe Beacon, 9 km south-west along the Icknield Way from Dunstable, a hilltop fortification built in the late Bronze Age is the forerunner of many others in the centuries to come.

The many "hoards" abandoned in the late Bronze Age (e.g. one from Wymington, Beds., containing over fifty axes) show that the bottom had fallen out of the market for bronze tools: it was no longer worthwhile to return and reclaim the scrap which had been buried for safety. A new metal had arrived, cheaper and tougher than any previously known: iron.

Fig. 14. Bronze Sword Blade found in Totternhoe (Scale 1:4).

Chapter 4

The Iron Age and the Celts

The Celts

Sometime after 1,000 B.C. a migration of peoples began to affect Europe. Greek and Roman writers called them Gauls or Celts. Their numbers grew steadily in central Europe for several hundred years, until in 399 B.C. a great army of Gauls under a chief named Brennus crossed the Alps, defeated the Roman army and captured the city of Rome.

Livy has recorded a romantic, ancient tale of how the grave Roman senators sat silent and motionless in their seats as the barbarians walked among them, plucking the senators' long beards to see if they were really alive, and of how the cackling of the sacred geese saved the Capitol, the Citadel of Rome, from a surprise assault. Rome survived and cleared the Gauls from Italy proper, though they settled in the Valley of the Po in northern Italy. They gave their name to the district which is now called Lombardy; to the Romans it was Cisalpine Gaul – Gaul this side of the Alps.

This was the year when Socrates died, when Plato was a young man, Euripides old, and Aristophanes in his prime; the glory of Ancient Greece was at its height and still expanding.

The Gauls also spread to other lands; the movement that sent Brennus from central Europe into Italy also sent offshoots of the same peoples to the north and west.

The Greek and Roman writers tell us where and when they settled in the Mediterranean; they give a view of what they were like. Livy thus described the Gauls who took Rome:

> "...of all the peoples who inhabit Asia the Gauls stand first in reputation for war.
> Among peoples of the most unwarlike sort this fierce tribe, travelling up and down in war, has almost made the world its residence. Tall bodies, long reddish hair, huge shields, very long swords. They go into battle with yells and leapings and the most dreadful din of arms as they clash shields according to some ancestral custom – all these are deliberately used to terrify their foes."

The only way we can define the Celts in these early historic times is to say that they were people speaking a Celtic language. In the century around the birth of Christ, Celtic languages were spoken in many parts of Europe, including France (Gaul) and Britain. The surviving descendants of these languages are Irish and Scottish Gaelic, Welsh and Breton. From this we know that at some time before the birth of Christ substantial numbers of

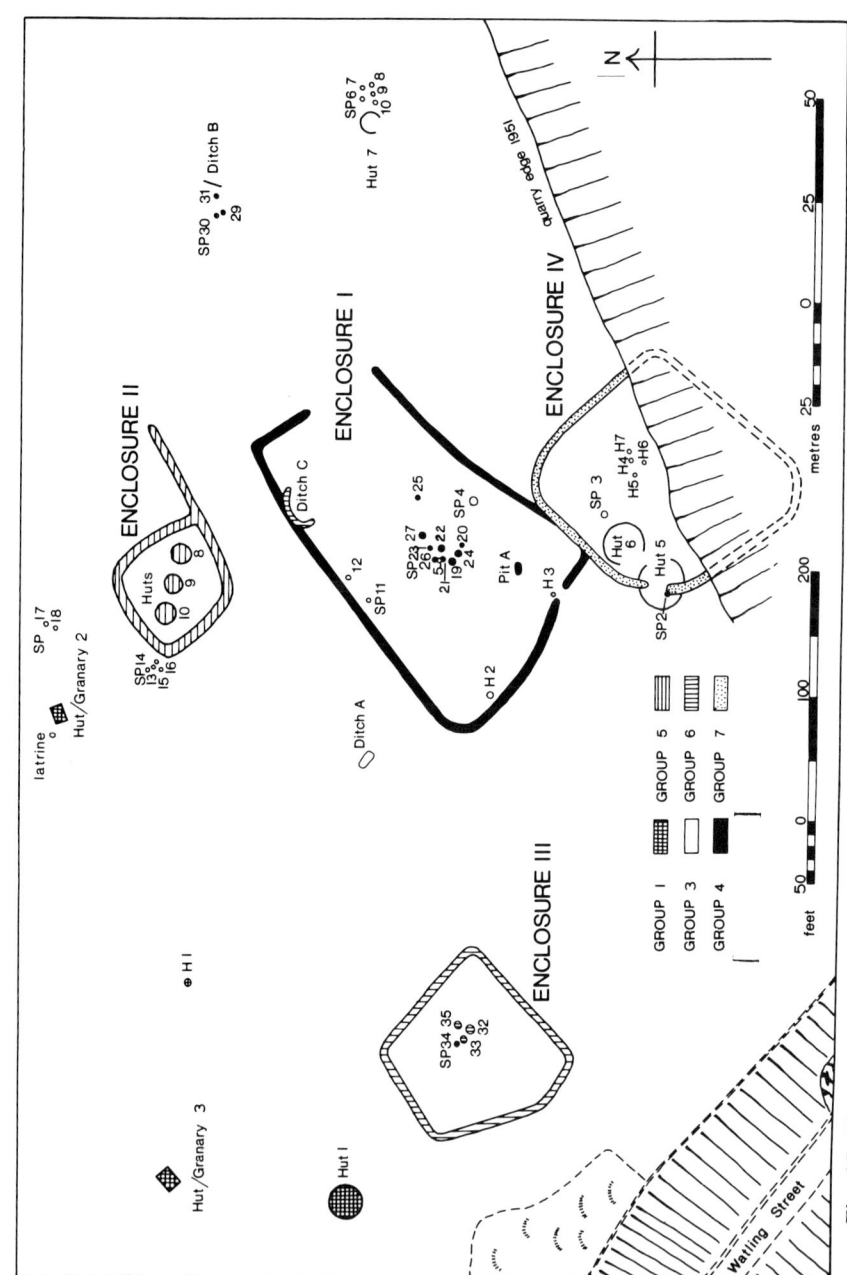

Fig. 15. Plan of Iron Age Features on Puddlehill. Hut 1 is First Iron Age House; Hut 5 is Second Iron Age House.

settlers must have come to Britain, bringing their Celtic language with them. It is not known when this was – writing was unknown to them, so they left no record – but it cannot have been later than some time during what we call the "Iron Age", when the use of iron became widespread in Britain.

There is no sudden change in the way of life of the people living in the Dunstable area. It is difficult to distinguish the pottery of the Late Bronze Age sites from that of the first settlement we have called "Iron Age". It has already been noted that the hillfort on Ivinghoe Beacon was built in the Bronze Age. The earliest fortification of Maiden Bower may be nearly as early, but it was certainly used and re-fortified during the Iron Age.

The date of transition to the general use of iron in Britain is now placed between 800 B.C. and 600 B.C.

The First Iron Age Farmstead on Puddlehill

On the top of the downland ridge of Puddlehill, on the northern outskirts of Dunstable, it has been possible to excavate very thoroughly a farmstead site that was occupied on and off throughout the Iron Age; that is from before 600 B.C. up to the Roman invasion (43 A.D.) and on through the period of Roman rule.

The Iron Age farmers chose this windswept site at Dunstable because it was probably already cleared of scrub by the previous inhabitants. The thin soil on the chalk is well drained and is good land for growing grain. It also had an adjacent water supply in a good spring that still rises from the foot of the hill to form the Ouzel, a tributary of the River Ouse.

These first settlers lived in a large, round house (Fig. 16). It had a diameter of 9 m marked as a circle of holes, showing where the posts of the structure had stood. By studying the size of the postholes we know that it was a sturdy building that housed this family of farmers. The outer timbers were tree trunks up to 30 cm in diameter. The roof was conical with a thick reed or straw thatch, and the walls would be made from either hides, wattle and daub, or stacked turves.

Such a building would be highly inflammable, and fires for heating and cooking would be a great hazard. To overcome this the hearths were contained in two small pits (B and C on the plan) near the centre of the hut, the smoke finding its way out through the rafters and thatch. Clay ovens were used for baking and one of these was found as a mass of collapsed burnt clay in a small pit also in the centre of the house (marked D on the plan).

At the Chiltern Open Air Museum at Chalfont St. Giles an Iron Age house has been built based on the plan of this one excavated on Puddlehill (Pl. 2).

The sausage-shaped hollow marked "A" on the plan is a feature often found in the houses of these people. Its use is unknown, but it may have been lined with hides to hold water, either for washing or for some form of

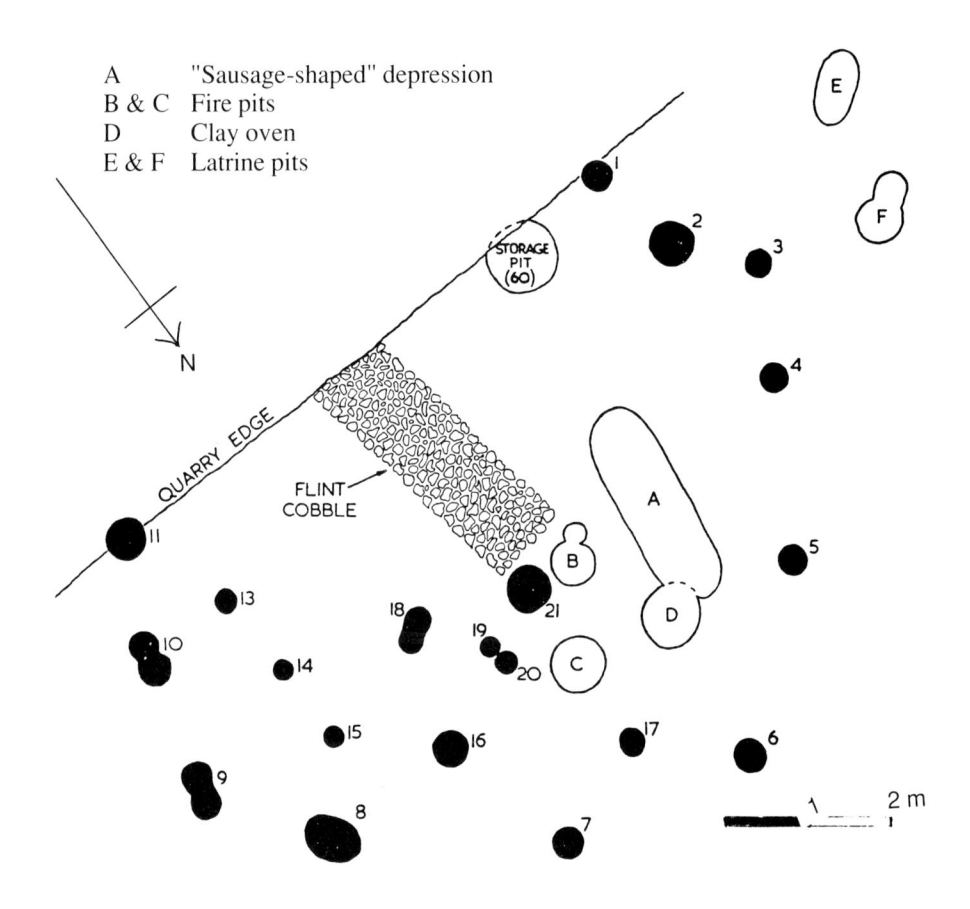

A   "Sausage-shaped" depression
B & C   Fire pits
D   Clay oven
E & F   Latrine pits

Fig. 16. First Iron Age House on Puddlehill

domestic processing – it is anyone's guess. The smaller post-holes inside the hut represent internal furnishings such as racks, platforms and perhaps a simple loom.

The path of flint cobbles leading to the hearth seems to suggest that the Iron Age housewife did not appreciate muddy boots fouling the rush or hide-strewn floor. It is true to say that these early people practised hygiene. They took the trouble to build latrine pits (E and F on the plan).

The round pit inside the house was a bell-shaped hole carved a metre deep into the solid chalk. This may have been used as the "pantry" for the store of their bread grain.

Plate 2. Iron Age house constructed at the Chiltern Open Air Museum. This is based on the First Iron Age Farmstead on Puddlehill.

As well as the round house, there were two rectangular structures of a kind often interpreted as being granaries for storing the harvest above ground as protection against vermin. Evidence for these buildings was found on Puddlehill as groups of postholes set apart from the farmhouse.

One showed a pattern of postholes of a building 3 m long and 2.2 m wide. Some of the postholes had been renewed like those of the house, suggesting a fairly long life.

The other was of a different kind. There were four postholes 1.2 m apart, each one cut to take 20 cm diameter posts. Later it seems this granary needed enlarging, and a new one was built on the same site. Larger posts were used and these were put 2.45 m apart. We can tell that this building was covered by a wide spreading roof by tracing the drip marks made by rain in the chalk.

Apparently the shelter made by this building standing on four stout uprights had also been used as a working place. A small hearth and various light stake holes were found beneath it, and flint cobbles had been used when the surrounding earth had been puddled into mud.

There was another hearth pit in use some distance from the house, and more of these hearths, used by later settlers on the site, were also found scattered around the hilltop. These were round pits up to 2 m in diameter sunk approximately 35 cm deep in the chalk. In the centre of each pit there were usually signs of burning, and in two of them we found large broken

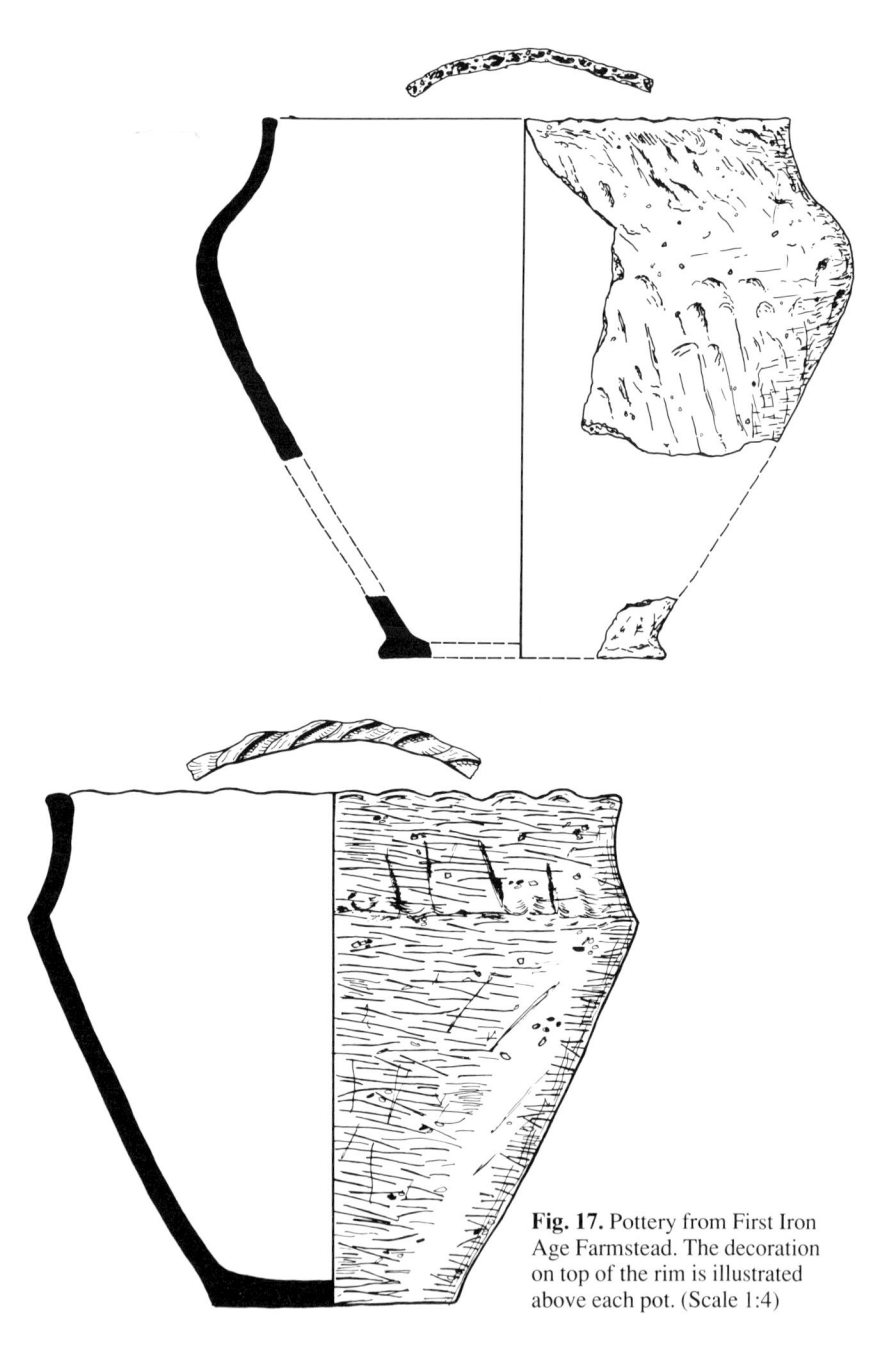

Fig. 17. Pottery from First Iron Age Farmstead. The decoration on top of the rim is illustrated above each pot. (Scale 1:4)

saddle querns which had apparently been used as hob stones. If you sat on the ground with your feet in the pit, they provided quite a comfortable position for cooking, and with a matting windbreak and a log backrest, would be a suitable place to leave the old folk to tend the family stewpot!

Diet and Way of Life

Two early varieties of wheat called Emmer and Spelt were grown in Britain in the Iron Age, and barley was also grown.

The grain was ground into flour by pouring it on to a large flat stone and grinding it with a flattened pebble. We have found many of these so called "bun" stones (Fig. 24). They are usually fashioned from sandstone and can be recognised by the gloss on the grinding surface. The flat mill stones or querns became worn with constant use into a saddle shape, hence the archaeologist's name for them of "saddle quern". These were usually of hard gritstone imported to the site, but they also used slabs of hard sandstone which were probably obtained from the region of Leighton Buzzard.

Bread produced in this manner must have been full of grit and hard on the teeth. The kind of loaf they produced can be seen in Plate 8. This loaf or bread roll was made by one of the later groups of Iron Age people on Puddlehill and survived because it was dropped into the hot ashes of a hearth and so became carbonised. Fortunately for the archaeologist, carbon, like the baked clay of pottery, is practically indestructible, and the flour and whole barley grains in this bread were perfectly preserved. Another staple food of the period was the "Celtic bean", a relative of the field bean and broad bean, but no evidence for this survived on Puddlehill.

The Iron Age people supplemented their main diet of beans and gritty bread with perhaps cheese and milk from their goats and cattle, and sweetening was probably provided by honey from wild bees. Meat was a luxury. We found very few animal meal bones amongst their refuse, but one reason for this may be that bone was a useful raw material and would often have been used for making tools rather than thrown away with the rubbish. The bones found were almost always from very young animals. They raised a few head of cattle, and kept pigs and sheep or goats. They may not have known how to make silage (though one pit found belonging to a later Iron Age occupation could have been for silage) and they had little winter fodder, so that it was difficult to carry stock over the winter. Young animals were therefore killed for food in the autumn. Britain at this time must have been well stocked with wild animals, but the people were not hunters and few meal bones of wild animals have been found in their refuse pits. They trapped small birds, probably larks, for which Dunstable has always been noted, and also collected fresh water mussels. Frog bones have been found in pits on the site, but we cannot tell whether these were from creatures which fell in and could not escape, or whether the inhabitants enjoyed frogs as a delicacy.

They tilled their fields with simple ploughs. The iron plough-share from one of these was found in a pit, and it is a simple blade with a socket (Fig. 24).

They have left us very few iron objects. If they had been there, we would undoubtedly have found them since iron seems to survive very well in chalk subsoil. The inference is that iron was a commodity only acquired by bartering, and people living on such a meagre economy had very little surplus for trade with the travelling "tinkers".

Simple flint scrapers and knives were found mixed with their rubbish, but these may have been left behind on the ground by earlier Neolithic or Bronze Age peoples.

The Iron Age farmers could work flint with skill when required, as is shown by the number of round hammer stones found. These were fashioned from flint to make perfectly round balls that vary from the size of a tangerine to that of a cricket ball. What they were used for we do not know but they were thrown away after the whole of the surface had been bruised by hammering. They are so common that they must have been in almost daily

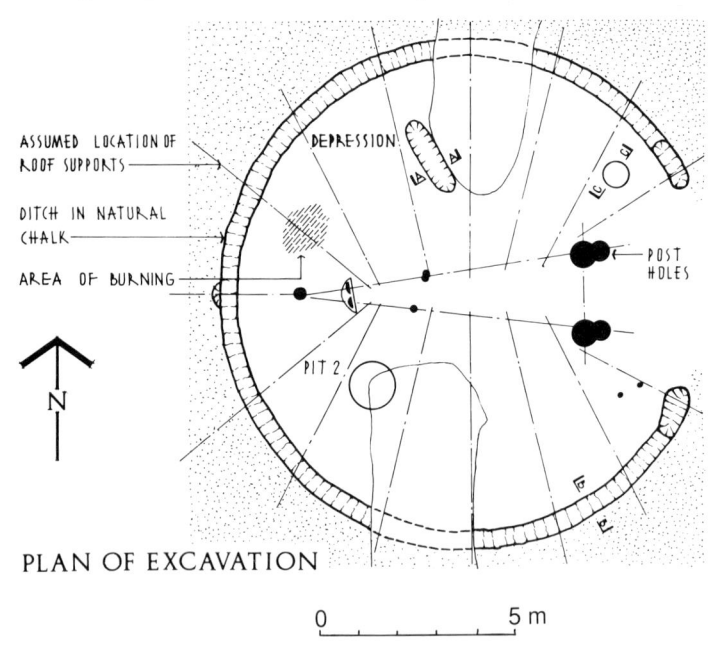

Fig. 18. Second Iron Age House on Puddlehill.

use, possibly for striking fire. To control the sparks a definite point of impact would be needed which could be obtained by using a spherical ball gripped firmly in the palm of the hand. By twisting the ball slightly a new striking point could be obtained for each blow.

How the people dressed we do not know, but it certainly was not only woad and skins. Within their huts and pits we find the loom weights and spindle whorls of weavers (Fig. 24). The spindle whorls were sometimes made by baking the local clay and sometimes they were carved from chalk. These chalk or clay discs had a hole pierced in the centre into which was inserted a stick. Attached to the stick was the raw wool or flax to be spun into thread. The weight of the spindle whorl provided the momentum to spin the stick and so twist the fibre into yarn. The weaving was carried out on upright looms, and to keep the warp threads taut, a series of weights was suspended along the bottom of the loom. It is these weights that were found on the site. Sometimes they were triangular with a hole pierced across each corner for the adjusting rope, and sometimes they were oblong with the hole pierced top and bottom. They were all easily made from local clay, and thrown away when the people moved site, new ones being made as required. On Puddlehill we found one that had gone wrong during manufacture. A pebble had been left in the clay and when the stick was pushed in to make the hole, it had struck the pebble. The maker of these weights had been sitting next to a fire and had thrown the thing down so that it became partially baked and so survived to illustrate this simple activity.

Experiment at the Butser Ancient Farm has shown that the soil does not become impoverished with continuous cultivation, particularly if manure from the animals is used. Nevertheless, the occupation on Puddlehill was not permanent: whatever the reason, the people moved away from the site from time to time. Eventually, after some years, another group would return, and it is this cycle of occupation that we have been able to observe by digging on Puddlehill.

With each re-occupation – although the way of life remained the same – small changes took place. Succeeding generations built their houses differently and changes also took place in the manufacture of pottery.

From the features found it would seem that the first settlement was a single family group living on an open site with apparently no enemies to disturb their economy.

Pottery and hearths of this period have also been found above Shirral Spring at Sewell, near the spring below Totternhoe Knolls and also overlooking the spring at Wellhead, but these sites have not been excavated so thoroughly as Puddlehill.

The Pottery

Fashions in pottery changed in prehistoric times just as they change today and, as we can recognise the patterns of our grandparents' bone china, so it is possible to distinguish the changing styles of the Iron Age. Despite the fact that each tribal group made its own pots from local sources of clay, and each pot was the work of an individual, certain pot shapes were common over very wide areas and their evolution can be recognised.

The earliest Iron Age pottery (Fig. 17), as already mentioned, shows little difference from that of the late Bronze Age. It was made from a chalky clay heavily tempered with crushed flint grit. It was made on the site, probably fired in an open hearth, and the potters pulled the wet clay into shape with their hands. A wheel for throwing pots was not used until the first century B.C.

The Second Farmstead

The next people to build their homes on the hill were still living on an open, undefended site, but there is a distinct change in the pottery techniques

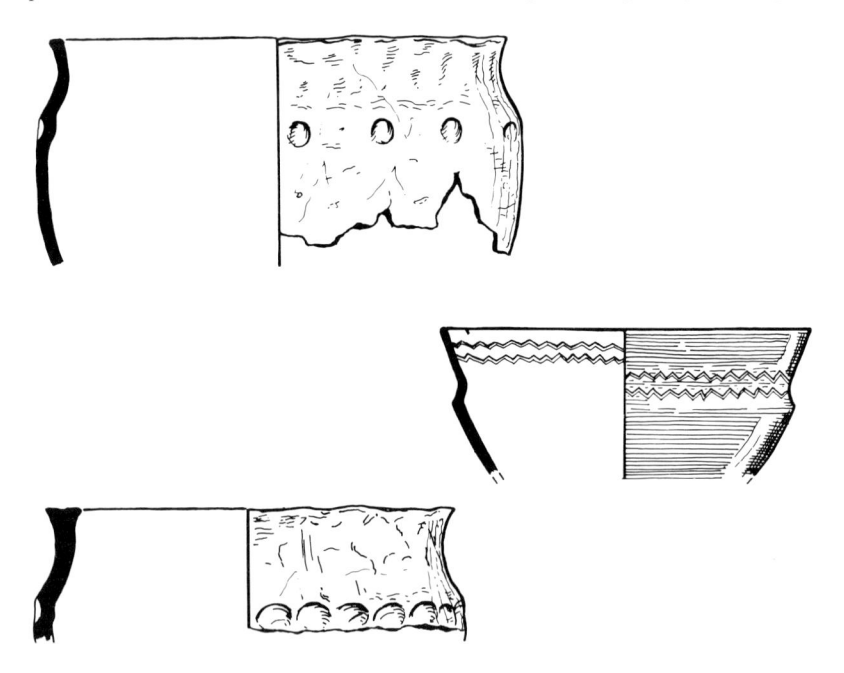

Fig. 19. Pottery from the Second Iron Age Farmstead (Scale 1:4). Two pots with finger-tip decoration, and a carinated bowl.

Plate 3. Carinated bowls. Fragments of good quality pottery from Second Iron age farmstead.

compared with those of the earlier inhabitants and this shows that a different people, or people of a different generation, now occupied the hilltop.

A new vessel appeared with this second occupation (Plate 3). This is sometimes called a "carinated bowl" from the carination, or keel, around the shoulder. These pots were beautifully made with a smooth paste and were highly polished. This polished surface was obtained by burnishing the clay pot with a piece of bone or a stone prior to firing. The decoration is usually in the form of triangles or zig-zags scratched on to the pot after it had been fired. These scratches were sometimes filled with white paint to provide a contrast against the jet black pot. Decoration on a number of the larger vessels was made by impressing the fingertip or fingernail into the pot while the clay was still wet (Fig. 19). From the size of these fingerprint impressions it is generally thought that the women of the tribe were the potters.

This pottery belongs to a style of manufacture which appeared in the Upper Thames region and the Chilterns in the 5th century B.C.

The plan of a house used on Puddlehill during this period is illustrated (Fig. 18). There were two of these and they were so large that they must have been communal dwelling places or accommodated an extended family. The house illustrated had a diameter of 11.6 m with a wide entrance facing eastwards away from the prevailing winds. The outer wall was found as a trench sunk 46 cm deep into the natural chalk with a few flints at the sides which gave way to a dark loam in the centre. It is the sameness of fill throughout the length, and the unweathered condition of the sides of the trench, that lead us to assume that it was built to contain a solid wall of close-set timbers rather than a series of separate posts. The loam fill in the centre was probably the remains of the rotted posts and this suggests that round timbers up to 23 cm in diameter had been used, and on this assumption 108 such posts would be required to provide the wall. Very little stone packing to these posts was found, and it is reasonable to suppose that the timbers of the wall stood no more than 90 cm above the ground level, and the excavated chalk was rammed hard down around the uprights. This would have been sufficient to provide a rigid construction capable of supporting heavy trusses and the weight of any type of roof.

The roof was supported inside the structure by six uprights. Three of these had been replaced or reinforced, suggesting repairs during the life of the building. One of the postholes at the back of the house carried two uprights of half round timbers. These could be seen in the hard-packed chalk as two half-moons of dark loam. The marks of these rotted posts were so clear that measurements could be taken to show that they had been made from a single tree trunk that originally had a diameter of 23 cm. This had been split down the centre to provide two poles.

The unusually wide entrance leads to doubts whether this structure was indeed a house at all. However, perhaps it was a deliberate feature to let in the light, and it is significant that just within the doorway, but under the shelter of the roof, was found evidence of working places. On one side of the entrance were twin postholes, perhaps built to carry the frame of a loom, and on the other side was a shallow pit which may have been the place where the corn was ground into flour. This pit was a shallow bowl worn into the virgin chalk, 13 cm deep with sharply incurved sides and a flat bottom. It was a perfect circle with a diameter of 69 cm, and the chalk was so smooth and symmetrical that it must have been worn into shape by friction. The continuous movement of a saddle quern under pressure of a rubbing stone may have produced this polished finish.

Other features of the interior furnishing of the house included a sausage-shaped depression as in the earlier house, and also a bell-shaped pit. This pit was unusual in that it had been lined with clay. It was sunk a metre deep into the chalk, the sides were slightly undercut and the flat bottom was covered with burnt material which included scraps of burnt bone, fire-crackled flints, and ash. Above this was a pile of baked clay debris which appeared to be the crumbled lining. The pit had smooth sides for the top 45 cm, but below this it had been left rough-hewn, presumably to provide a key for the clay. Its probable use was as a cooking place which

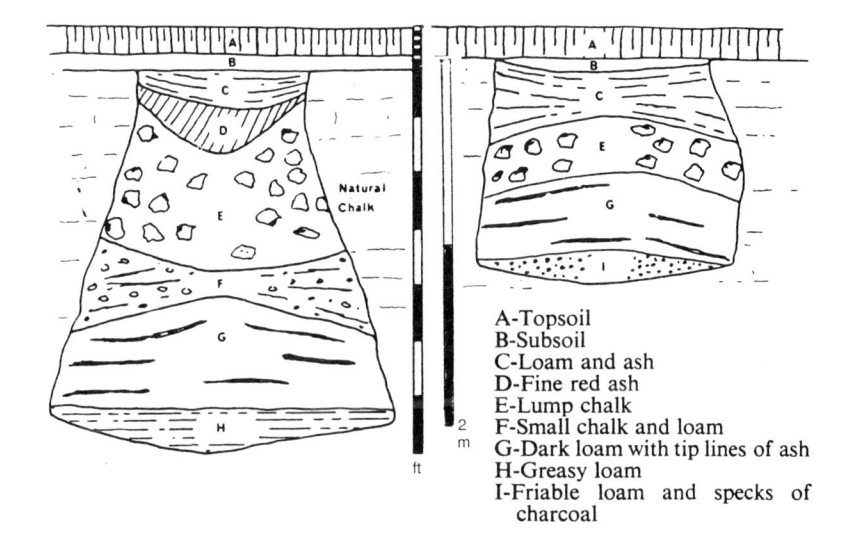

A-Topsoil
B-Subsoil
C-Loam and ash
D-Fine red ash
E-Lump chalk
F-Small chalk and loam
G-Dark loam with tip lines of ash
H-Greasy loam
I-Friable loam and specks of charcoal

Fig. 20. Sections through two Storage Pits.

would serve the dual purpose in winter of providing the hut with central heating. The technique used would be to put charcoal and hot stones into the pit with the food to be baked and then with the top sealed, to allow the food to cook in a slow and gentle heat. This method of cooking was in use on the site several centuries later during the Romano-British period, and as a cooking method it has lasted until recent times in the sand ovens of South Wales and similar charcoal ovens used by the Yorkshire housewife to bake bread.

No hearth as such was found in this hut, but a few fragments of fire-crackled flints and a discoloration of the chalk showing signs of fire were found on the side away from the door. This may have been the site of an open hearth.

There were seven hearth pits of the kind also used by the first Iron Age farmers on Puddlehill. Among the ashes was found part of a deer antler with the tines cut off and also, blackened by fire, the top of a human skull.

Storage Pits

The people living in these round houses had no rectangular "granaries". Their grain, and perhaps other foodstuffs, were stored in deep pits. These pits are a characteristic feature of the Iron Age, and their use lasted until the advent of the late pre-Roman Iron Age people (sometimes called the "Belgae") in the first century B.C.

The pits were found scattered all over the occupation site, sometimes singly and sometimes in groups, according to the size of the community living on the hill at one time. They varied slightly in shape and size throughout the centuries, but were essentially either barrel or bell shaped, to provide the maximum storage capacity with the smallest possible aperture for ease of covering.

Two types are illustrated (Fig. 20). The deeper pits would require a ladder for exit and entry. Pit 1 was over 2 m deep and 2 m wide at the bottom, but the mouth measured only 1 m across. A small oval was worn into one side of the top of this pit showing where a single pole ladder had rested.

Experiments in the storage of grain in pits have been carried out at the Butser Ancient Farm Research Project in Hampshire. The corn was threshed and, without drying, poured into the pit to fill it completely. The top of the pit was tightly sealed with a layer of clay, which was then covered with soil to keep the clay moist so that rain would not penetrate through cracks. Stored in this way, with or without a wicker lining in the pit, the grain keeps

Plate 4. Skeleton in storage pit.

well through the winter and can be used the following year either for food or for seed corn. An average-sized pit holds more than a tonne of corn.

The grains of corn take in oxygen and give off carbon dioxide, and once the pit is sealed the carbon dioxide collects in it, excluding oxygen, and the crop is preserved in a dormant state. There is an initial loss of the grain nearest the outside: about two per cent of the total. The remainder of the crop is well preserved, so long as the temperature remains fairly low and the rainfall is not heavy enough to leak in through the sides of the pit.

When these pits are found by archaeologists they are usually full of household rubbish and therefore provide much information about the way of life at the time. Since experiments show that pits could be used year after year for food storage, it is puzzling to know why they were abandoned and used for depositing refuse.

When we emptied pits like these on Puddlehill we found that in the winter frosts caused the tops and sides to cave in. From the weathered chalk found in the pits it is possible to make a reasonable estimate as to the time of year when they were finally abandoned. Those that were discarded during the hard weather of winter were almost full of small chalk and contained very little camp rubbish. Those that were emptied during late spring or early summer retained their original shape and were filled with household refuse before the frosts could attack the chalk sides. Other pits fell between these two extremes, and the layers of camp debris were interleaved with weathered chalk. One of the pits was obviously emptied during the early summer and filled completely before winter with kitchen refuse and ash from the hearths. This lay in "tip lines" throughout the filling.

Some of the pits were left with the sides rough-hewn, still showing the original pick marks. As there is no wear on the sides of these pits they may have been lined. Some support for this is the finding of mouse skeletons on the floor. One can imagine them hiding beneath the lining when the last grain was shovelled out by someone standing within the pit. Pit 1 is this type, with pick marks showing on the side of the pit and mouse skeletons on the floor. In crevices at the bottom of two of the pits we have found a few grains of carbonised wheat which provides supporting evidence for their use as grain stores.

One pit held a more grisly find: crouched face-down in a position which suggested her hands had been tied together, was the skeleton of a young woman. On her left leg lay a horse skull, and just below her chest was a squared block of chalk. Otherwise, the contents of the pit were the usual camp rubbish. This was certainly not the regular form of burial at the period, though similar cases of bodies in pits have been found elsewhere. Was she buried alive? The horse skull is sometimes connected with witchcraft: was she a witch? or a criminal? or perhaps a murder victim? or a human sacrifice, like the bodies sometimes found in bogs?

Plate 5. Aerial photograph of Maiden Bower.

Apart from this hint of violence these early occupations seem to suggest a people living peaceably. We have found no weapons, unless one includes the numerous stones and pebbles found on the site. These are foreign to this chalk Down, but since most of those associated with the early people show signs of burning, they are more likely to have been used as pot boilers – heated in the fire and dropped into the pot to boil water.

No enclosure ditches have been found; no remains of dogs that would give warning of the approach of strangers; no pens to corral the stock against cattle thieves – only the evidence of small communities eking a frugal existence from their shallow soil, living at peace with their neighbours, with no fear of intruders stealing their few cattle or their stocks of grain.

Similar open farm sites have also been found on the high ridge at Eggington, on the ridge at Billington and on Pitstone Hill.

Hillforts

The fortifications which crowned so many hilltops in the Iron Age, however, show that all was not peaceful. More than 1,300 of them have been identified in southern Britain. Perhaps the farmers on Puddlehill could flee to safety when danger threatened, within the ramparts of Maiden Bower?

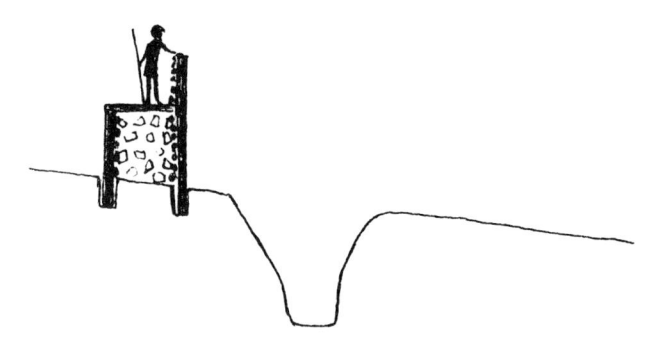

First fortification, based on that at Ivinghoe Beacon

Second fortification

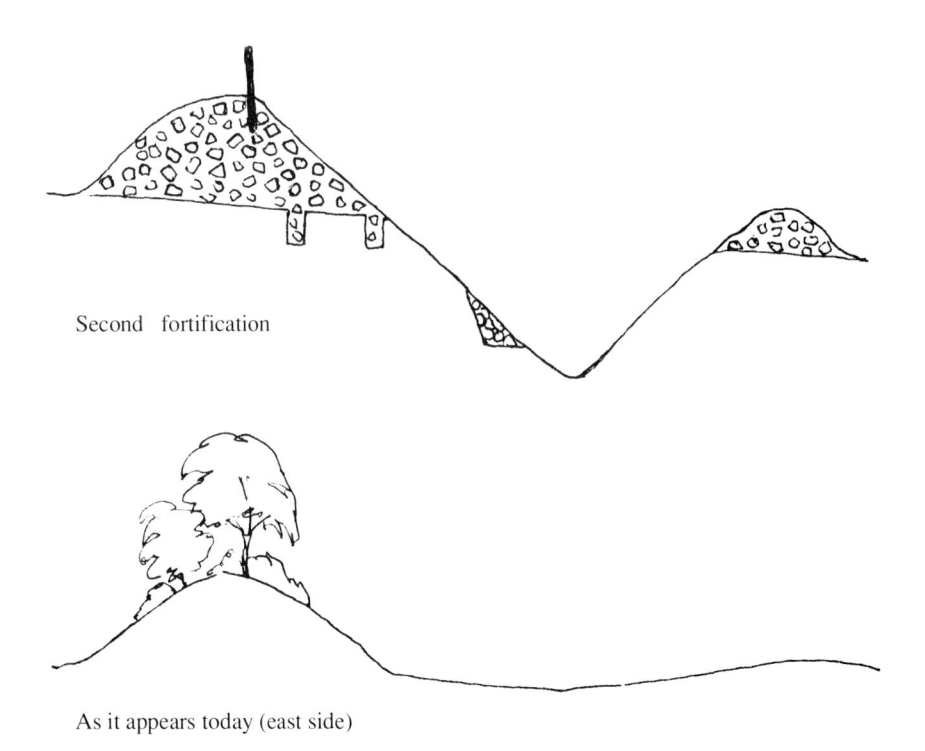

As it appears today (east side)

Fig. 21. Maiden Bower Iron Age Fort. Sections through rampart and ditch.

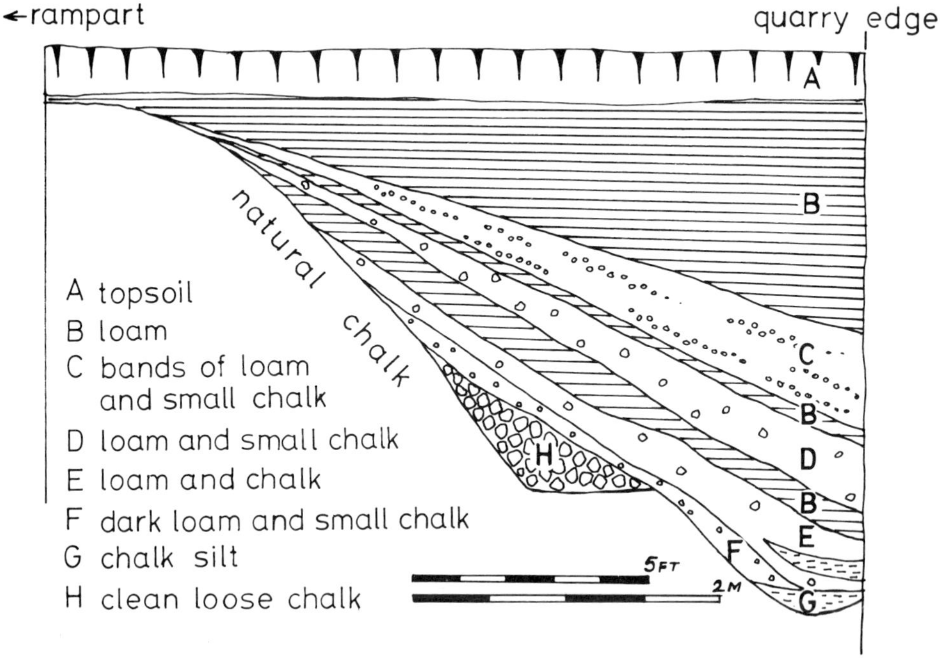

←rampart quarry edge

A topsoil
B loam
C bands of loam and small chalk
D loam and small chalk
E loam and chalk
F dark loam and small chalk
G chalk silt
H clean loose chalk

natural chalk

Fig. 22. Maiden Bower. Section through silted up ditch where it shows on edge of quarry. *H* is the bottom of the ditch of the first fortification.

It is not quite accurate to call this a "hillfort" since it is situated on the edge of a plateau, with a slope on only one side where the chalk quarry now lies. It has a good all-round view and it lies partly over the Neolithic causewayed enclosure constructed more than 2,000 years earlier. This spot might have had some kind of sacred significance: shrines have been identified in some hillforts, although their principal purpose was obviously defensive.

The earliest hillfort in our own area was built on the highest point of Ivinghoe Beacon. A ditch was dug following the contour of the hilltop, and the excavated chalk was thrown up to make a single rampart. This can still be seen today as a low grass-grown ridge surrounding the flat top of this landmark that stands high above the surrounding countryside.

The other strategically placed hillfort in the district is Ravensburgh Castle in the hills to the south of Hexton. This occupies a natural ridge of ground protected on three sides by deep ravines. Excavation has shown that it was constructed and re-fortified during the Iron Age. There is another fort at Wilbury Hill just outside Letchworth. Further hillforts are found northwards into Northamptonshire and westwards along the edge of the chalk scarp into

Plate 6. Maiden Bower. Post-holes of the Iron Age Hillfort dug into a ditch of the Neolithic Causewayed Camp. Chalk from the rampart has slipped into the holes, so that they show up white against the dark ditch-fill.

Buckinghamshire and along the Thames. Southwards there is a fort called "the Aubreys" at Redbourn (visible from the M1). However, there is very little material of Iron Age date recorded in the area roughly bounded by the River Thames, the River Lea, the Icknield Way and Watling Street.

Maiden Bower, about one and a half kilometres from the Puddlehill settlement, has never been excavated, but a chalk quarry has eaten its way into the ditch and rampart on the northern side; from observations carried out during many years of erosion of this quarry edge, we do now know something about its construction (Fig. 21). It measures within its ramparts 229 m from east to west and 236 m from north to south enclosing approximately ten acres (about 4 hectares). The banks still stand as an inverted V, in some places over 2 m high, and originally it was surrounded by a ditch. The silted fill of the ditch and the old land surface beneath the rampart can plainly be seen on the quarry edge. Beneath the rampart we have found a series of holes 2–3 m apart that once carried large posts to hold the rampart in position. The holes have diameters of 25 cm to 30 cm and all are approximately 90 cm deep (as far as an arm can reach). The sides were smooth but showed that a flat 5 cm wide blade had been used to cut them.

They were apparently "tailor-made" to fit round uprights. The filling of the holes was chalk with small flecks of charcoal increasing towards the bottom of each hole, showing how each post had rotted as it stood, the hole gradually filling with the clean excavated chalk that made up the rampart. Where the postholes had been dug through the fill of one of the Neolithic ditches they show up white against the dark silt (Plate 6).

There were rows of posts at the front and back of the rampart, with the chalk excavated from the surrounding ditch piled between them to form a defensive wall (Fig. 21). When the fort was originally constructed the ditch was dug with a very steep inner face. Any attacker had to face an enemy entrenched behind this ditch and a vertical wall of chalk and timber. This was the method of construction called a "box rampart", used at Ivinghoe Beacon and many other hillforts, but at some later date in the Iron Age a new type of defence was developed and Maiden Bower was re-fortified in the new fashion. This meant re-cutting the ditch as a deep, wide V, obliterating most of the earlier ditch, which had had very steep sides and a narrow flat bottom. The new rampart was a simple "dump" with sloping sides which did not require supporting timbers, though it probably had a wooden palisade on the top. An attacker was faced by a continuous slope from the bottom of the ditch to the top of the rampart. It is possible that this re-fortification was never completed: there is some evidence that the wider ditch does not completely circle the fort.

In any case it was probably attacked very shortly after it had been built. Along the bottom of the ditch that has now been eaten away by the quarry we have found hundreds of sling stones. These are river-rolled pebbles about the size of a walnut and are only found in the bottom of the ditch, having been thrown there before any weathering of the freshly excavated chalk had taken place, i.e. within a few weeks.

We have also found in the bottom of the ditch evidence of a massacre. The skeleton of an adult was lying in the bottom of the ditch in a crouched position, and above were the skeletons of three adults who had been beheaded, and the skeleton of a baby. In the same length of ditch were the skeletons of two young people.

The three adults had been thrown into the ditch and were lying spread-eagled on the ditch sides. The neck vertebrae of one of them had been sliced cleanly in half by a single blow. The baby was probably only a few months old at the time of death and had been thrown into the ditch with the other people. The fact that two of the adult skulls were missing suggests the possibility that the heads were carried off as the spoils of battle. The covering of this gruesome slaughter was clean chalk that must have been taken from the rampart, and it looks as if the fort had been deliberately broken down at this point. These bodies were found at the eastern side of the quarry and there may be more to be discovered if the site is excavated.

Excavations of the interior of hillforts often uncover foundations of buildings, sometimes set closely along streets. These may be dwellings or store-houses. There are also usually storage pits, so it may be that surplus grain, or a tribute paid in produce to an overlord, was stored in safety within the ramparts. Greek and Roman writers tell us that Britain exported corn to the Continent in the last century B.C.

The only excavation carried out inside Maiden Bower was by the farmer Dan Cook, assisted by Worthington Smith, in 1913. This was just within the entrance, which is on the south side, and revealed a trench with a row of pits which may have held the posts of some kind of gateway. There was also a deep pit full of human bones, but these appear to have been buried in the Roman period, after Maiden Bower had ceased to be used as a fortification.

Very little datable material has been found in the ditches of Maiden Bower where they are gradually eroding on the face of the old chalk quarry, but one sherd of pottery is almost identical with one belonging to the second Iron Age occupation on Puddlehill. This suggests a link between the farmstead and the fort.

CHAPTER 5

The Middle Iron Age (c.300 B.C. - c.50 B.C.)

New Settlers on Puddlehill

Many years passed after the departure from Puddlehill of the farmers described in the previous chapter. Their pits and hearths had been lost to view by the time the area was re-settled by a new group of people, and there were noticeable differences in the way the newcomers organised their lives. From now on, enclosure ditches were dug to surround the dwellings, and also some of the storage pits, and the houses were no longer so substantial as the earlier ones.

The pottery style had changed: instead of angular shoulders and zig-zag decoration the pots now had rounded shapes. The crushed flint grit was replaced by sand as a filler in the clay, giving a smoother fabric, and increasingly it was burnished with a stone or bone to produce a shiny black

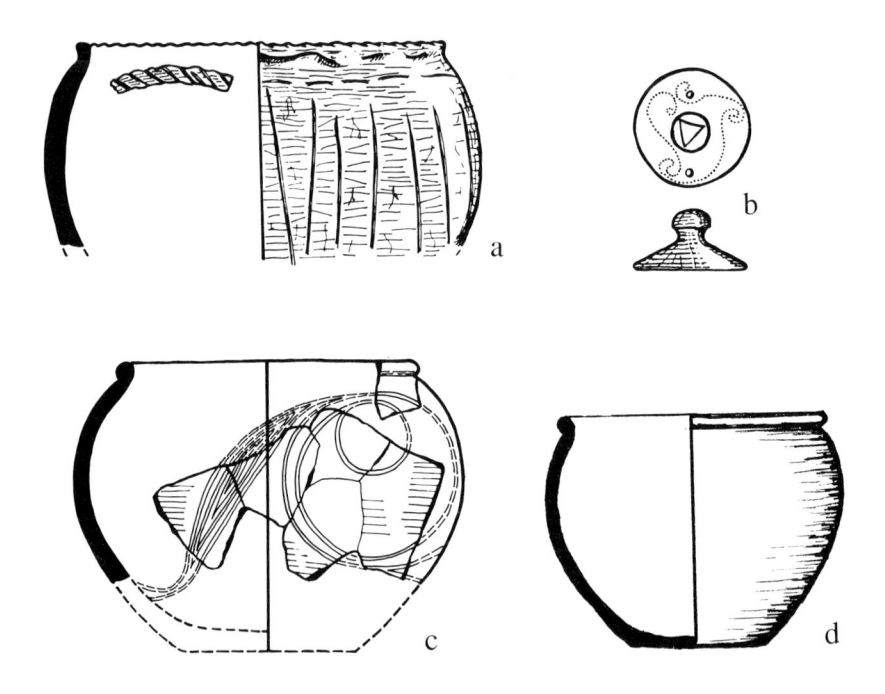

Fig. 23. Pottery of the Middle Iron Age Period, Puddlehill (Scale 1:4).

Plate 7. Decorated Pot-lid found in a Storage Pit.

surface. This not only gave an attractive appearance but also made the pot less porous. The unburnished vessels often had vertical grooves scratched on the surface (Fig. 23 *a*).

Some of the pots were beautifully decorated with curved scroll patterns (Fig. 23 and Plate 7) of a kind sometimes called "Celtic art" or "La Tène" (after a site in Switzerland). The decorated bowl and pot lid illustrated had the pattern impressed before firing. Both of these pieces, together with other sherds of the period, were of excellent manufacture showing highly developed techniques of firing. Associated with them were pots of very

Plate 8. Carbonised bread roll.

crude manufacture – the proportion of fine wares to coarse being equal. The pot lid is pierced like a modern teapot to allow the escape of steam. No pottery vessel small enough for this lid was found on the site, and it is to be presumed that it was made for a metal vessel that could be used on a fire.

The pottery from this period on Puddlehill is of a style not found much further east than Bedfordshire. Its appearance here is dated to about 300 B.C.

Enclosures, Houses and Pits

The first of these new occupations of the site was identified by a rectangular enclosure (I on Fig. 15), three quarters of an acre in size. This was marked by a V-shaped ditch approximately 1.5 m deep and 2 m wide. The chalk from the ditch had been thrown up on the inside to make a bank. The entrance on the west side was by a gated causeway. The two postholes that carried this gate were found one on either side set back an equal distance from the ditch ends. One of the postholes had been dug through an earlier hearth pit, and it is this kind of stratification that enables us to put the later date to this construction. The filling of this hearth had been a soft loam so a great number of stones had been used to pack and hold the post firm. These stones must have been collected from the surface of the site, for not only did they include three flint hammers, but also all of them showed some sign of previous use, either as hammer stones or stones that had been used as pot boilers or firestones. No traces of a gate were found across the wide entrance on the east side of this enclosure; it was probably closed by a hedge or fence of hurdles.

Within the enclosure was a group of storage pits. That these were contemporary with the ditch is shown by the finding of a few scraps of pottery in the lower levels of the ditch belonging to a pot which had been thrown into one of the abandoned pits.

No houses were found in the enclosure, but the amount of household refuse deposited in abandoned storage pits shows that the people must have been living close by. As well as pottery there were loomweights, a bone toggle and an iron saw (Fig. 24).

Another enclosure (II), perhaps contemporary with the first, contained three roughly circular houses. An innovation here was the use of the rotary quern for grinding corn. A shale bead was also found: the only piece of personal decoration discovered throughout the centuries of the Iron Age occupation of the hill. Within one of the dwellings was a small sharpening stone of hard igneous rock that had a hole pierced in one end so that the owner could suspend it from the waist, or carry it round the neck. There were also the burnt remains of a weaving comb decorated with a circle and dot pattern, and triangular and oblong loom weights.

The ditches and single bank of these enclosures were too small for defence against invaders, but would serve to deter the casual thief or perhaps to keep their cattle and stock away from the pits. The ditches appeared to have been kept very clean and the throwing of camp refuse into them must have been taboo. Very little chalk silt was allowed to accumulate in the bottom before they became grassed over, and this covering of vegetation preserved the shape of the ditch and laid down a stratum of rich loam that represents to the excavator the period in which the enclosure was occupied.

The vegetation covering the ditches would be grazed by the stock around the homestead and this continuous close cropping by the cattle and sheep would produce a fine springy turf. When the site was abandoned and the ditches no longer grazed, they would quickly become filled with lank, coarse vegetation which would be the home for countless snails. The banks would be overgrown and broken down with bushes. Consequently the ditch silting shows the occupation period as a rich loam layer and the period of non-occupation as a chalky loam fill in which snail shells form almost 50 per cent of the content. The snails are mainly of the species *Cepaea nemoralis* – a variety found in great numbers on the downs today, particularly in hollows or where the grass grows long and coarse.

This change in vegetation, illustrated in the prehistoric ditch fillings, has been noticeable on Dunstable Downs with the disappearance of sheep in our own lifetime. The once fine-textured turf, with its banks of thyme, is giving

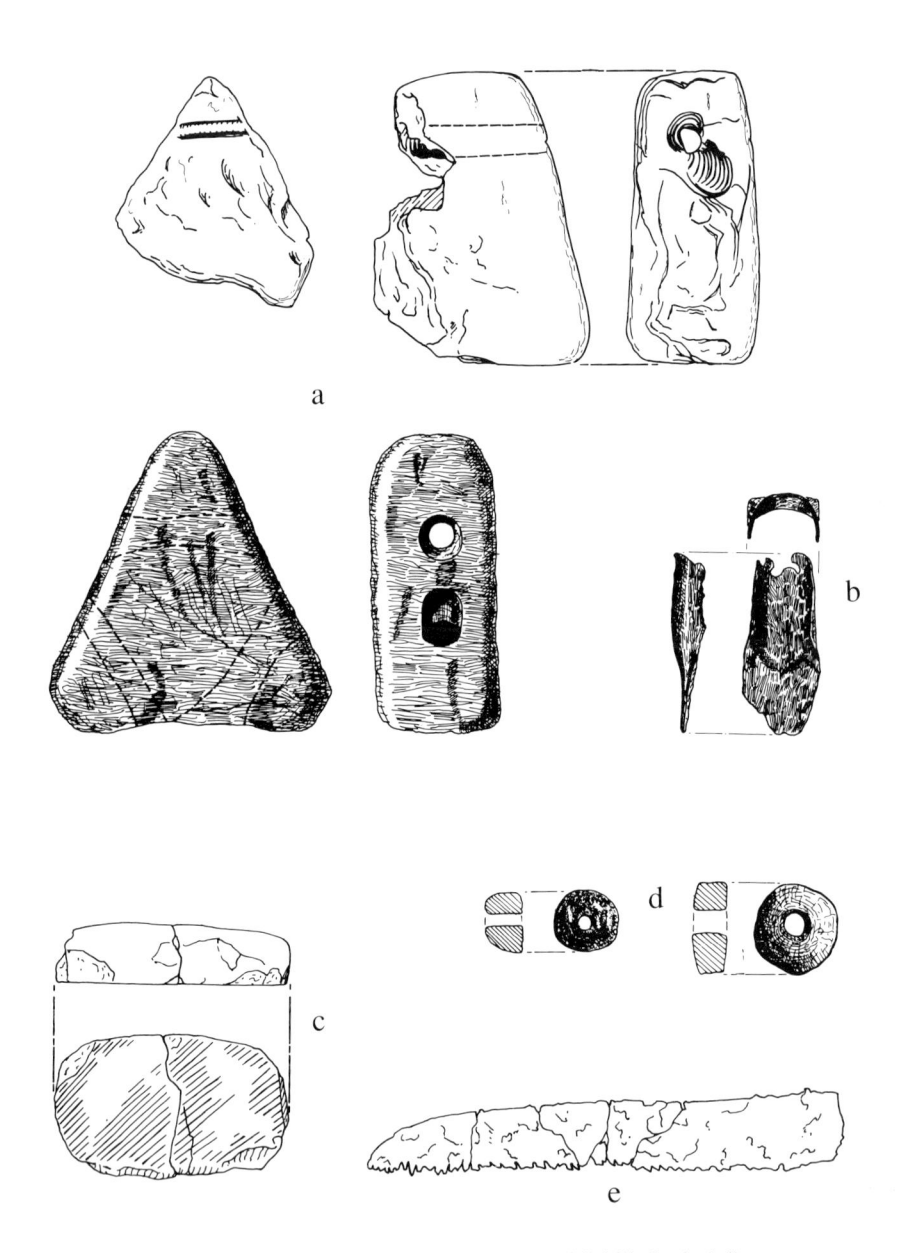

Fig. 24. Finds from the Middle Iron Age Farmstead, Puddlehill (Scale 1:4). *a*, Loomweights; *b*, Ploughshare; *c*, "Bun-stone" for grinding corn; *d*, Spindle Whorls; *e*, Saw.

way to the hawthorn bushes and coarse grasses. The hollows where children once romped are now overgrown and full of matted vegetation. A section cut through one of these hollows in a hundred years' time will show a similar fill to that in these enclosure ditches.

Very little rubbish is found in the lower levels of the enclosure ditches and although the lack of material evidence from them is disappointing, it does show that these people looked upon the task of ditch digging as a labour that was great enough for the ditch to be worth care and attention after it had been dug.

A third enclosure ditch (III) surrounded four more storage pits. As with Enclosure II there was no entrance and the ditch must have been bridged. The pottery fragments were similar to those already described from this period, but with an even higher proportion of shiny, burnished vessels (73 per cent). There were also some pots which appear to be home-made imitations of a new style of pottery introduced in the late pre-Roman Iron Age (see Chapter 6). This suggests a date in the first century B.C.

The site may have been abandoned before the empty storage pits became filled with camp refuse, for calcified tubers of earth nuts (*Bunium flexuosum*) were found in a stratum halfway down the pits. This herb still grows on the site and it must have taken several years for it to seed in the pits and develop the fully grown tubers in such quantity. This is evidence for a number of years without disturbance in this area.

A Response to Danger

The last Iron Age enclosure (IV) on Puddlehill was different from all the earlier ones: it was intended as a defence, but it was never finished. It would have contained an area of less than half an acre. At the single entrance the ditch was made 3 m wide and 2 m deep, the chalk being thrown up to make a simple rampart. A half circle of postholes was found between the ends of the ditch which must have formed some kind of defence at the entrance. At the back of the enclosure the ditch was excavated only 76 cm deep and 1 m wide. On the same ridge at Totternhoe some 2 km away the same thing happened: a ditch enclosing an

Fig. 25. Pot from Enclosure III, showing influence of Iron Age ("Belgic") style (Scale 1:4). Compare with Fig. 27 *f*.

even smaller area than on Puddlehill was made with a single entrance protected by a stout palisade. This ditch was also 3 m wide and 2 m deep at the entrance but along part of the enclosure, although it was marked out 3 m wide it had been dug only 30 cm deep when it was abandoned.

The scare that caused these farmers to dig these hasty defences either passed quickly or the inhabitants were overrun before they had time to finish them. Perhaps the only sign of violence was the finding in the deepest part of the Puddlehill ditch of the skeleton of a thirteen-year-old girl. She was lying in the bottom of the ditch and had not been buried in a grave. She was covered with snail shells and a light, chalky loam – a stratum that is associated with the natural silting of these ditches.

It is not easy to fix the date at which this happened. As in Enclosure III, one of the pots shows the influence of late Iron Age styles. The fact that the girl's body lay unburied while the silt of the ditch slowly covered her suggests that years passed before people lived on Puddlehill again.

Rulers and Religion

Nothing found near Dunstable gives a clue to the political organisation or the religious beliefs of the prehistoric people who lived there. During the two or three hundred years in which the middle Iron Age peoples lived on Puddlehill, there was very little change in their way of life and probably very little change in their political organisation.

The great sacred centres of the Neolithic and early Bronze Age such as Stonehenge and Avebury had fallen into disuse hundreds of years before; in later generations, when the Romans came, they found druids and bards with a venerable learning, respected and obeyed over a great part of Britain. It is likely that in the second century B.C. the druids already existed and knit together separate settlements into some kind of religious bond.

We do not know whether the local Iron Age farmers obeyed rulers or nobles. We do not know whether the hillforts were occupied occasionally or continuously, nor whether it was at the same time as the farms; if similar pottery were to be found in Maiden Bower to that in use on Puddlehill, but accompanied by jewellery or other items indicating wealth, then it would suggest that people richer and more powerful than their fellows lived there as rulers. On present evidence there is nothing to indicate that the Iron Age farmers of the Dunstable district were subject to chieftains, or formed any part of a political state.

CHAPTER 6

The Late Pre-Roman Iron Age

The Historical Record Begins

If little changed in Bedfordshire during the early and middle Iron Age, very much changed in Europe that was to transform Britain in the next century. Whilst the middle Iron Age people were living near the future site of Dunstable, in 203 B.C. the Romans defeated Hannibal of Carthage and made themselves masters of the whole of the western Mediterranean. Immediately they declared war on King Philip V of Macedon, whom they beat decisively in 197 B.C. Seven years later they defeated the King of Syria as thoroughly, and made themselves masters of the eastern as well as of the western Mediterranean. The conquering Romans absorbed the culture of the Greeks they subdued, and henceforth the civilization which they carried with them into central and western Europe was a Greco-Roman culture, heir to the traditions of Pericles and Socrates as well as to those of the ancient consuls of Rome.

Up to this time Britain and its inhabitants had been living beyond the knowledge of these classical peoples. Even the most learned bard or druid could not read or write, so that no written records were kept and anything we know about life in Britain at that time must come from archaeological discoveries.

In the last century before the birth of Christ this began to change. The people of northern Europe, including Britain, began increasingly to interest the writers of Greek and Latin. As Roman influence extended north and west it began to make itself felt even in the distant offshore islands of Britain and Ireland.

During this period gold coins called staters, originating in the mint of Philip II of Macedon (359–336 B.C.), found their way across Europe into Gaul. For over a century the Gaulish peoples copied these coins, and continued to make copies of the copies in more and more bizarre forms. Some time not long before 100 B.C. several kinds of Gaulish coins, with designs but without lettering, appeared in considerable numbers in southern Britain.

At the same time in Europe came the first migration of new peoples, speaking Germanic languages. These languages were the ancestors of modern German, English, Dutch and the Scandinavian languages.

The Belgae

Two Germanic peoples, known as the Teutones and the Cimbri, moved south in a great swarm from the peninsula that is now Denmark, bringing with them wives and children in lumbering wagons. They swept through

Gaul and entered Italy, where they were defeated in masterly fashion by the Roman General Marius. The only Gaulish people who were able to withstand and defeat the Germans were the Belgae, a group of tribes living in what is now north-eastern France and Belgium, who had already received some German settlers among them.

About the time of the German invasion, some Belgic colonists crossed the channel and settled in Britain. The date is uncertain, but coins of the Bellovaci and the Atrebates minted around 100 B.C. are found in some numbers in south-eastern Britain. Caesar, writing about 50 B.C., says that the Belgae withstood the Germans in "our fathers' time" and that the colonists still obeyed Divitiacus of the Suessiones (Soissons) "within living memory", i.e. twenty or thirty years earlier. The first colonists presumably crossed the channel some time before or after 100 B.C.

Julius Caesar: The Roman Expeditions to Britain

The first Roman venture into Britain came some fifty years or so after the colonists landed. In the aftermath of conquest, the old Roman constitution had collapsed and left Rome at the mercy of rival contenders for power. Caesar stood against Pompey. Whilst Pompey held the command of the army of Spain and stayed in Rome to control the politics of the Capital, Caesar took command of the army of Roman southern Gaul – the modern Provence. He made a great reputation for himself and eclipsed Pompey by a bold lightning conquest of the whole of Gaul. In the course of his campaigns he led two expeditions to Britain in 55 and 54 B.C.

To Romans, Britain was a half legendary land, entirely different from the rest of the world. In popular thought the world was round like a plate, with land in the centre, enclosing the safe Mediterranean – "our sea" – while beyond the land mass lay the turbulent outer ocean, spilling off the edges of the plate in a gigantic waterfall. In that outer ocean lay two considerable islands, namely Britain and Ceylon. In northern Britain the air was so poisonous that human beings could not survive, and to Britain at Midsummer Eve, unseen unearthly sailors ferried the souls of the dead. Caesar's raids, presented as a conquest of the island, could hardly have made a deeper impression on Roman public opinion if he had discovered America or annexed Mars!

Before Caesar, our knowledge of Britain is a matter of conjecture about how and when nameless people lived in a society whose essential outlines escape us. With the narrative of Caesar, written within three years of the event as an autobiography designed to hearten his supporters and confound the adherents of Pompey, we know the day and hour of the main events, the names of peoples he encountered and their chieftains, and much of their manner of living and fighting. Caesar's account of his invasions of Britain is the earliest surviving piece of written history concerning this Island to describe the Belgae and the other Britons. He tells us of their skill as charioteers:

> "In chariot fighting the Britons begin by driving all over the field hurling javelins, and generally the terror inspired by the horses and noise of the wheels are sufficient to throw their opponents' ranks into disorder. Then, after making their way between the troops of their own cavalry, they jump down from the chariots and engage on foot." He goes on to say "...by daily training and practice they attain such proficiency that even on a steep incline they are able to control the horses at full gallop, and to check and turn them in a moment. They run along the chariot pole, stand on the yoke, and get back into the chariot as quick as lightning.
>
> "...The interior of Britain is inhabited by people who claim, on the strength of an oral tradition, to be aboriginal; the coast, by Belgic immigrants – nearly all of them retaining the names of the tribes from which they originated – who came to plunder and make war and who later settled down to till the soil. The population is exceedingly large, the ground thickly studded with homesteads, closely resembling those of the Gauls, and the cattle very numerous. For money they use either bronze, or gold coins, or iron ingots of fixed weights. Tin is found inland, and small quantities of iron near the coast; the copper that they use is imported. There is timber of every kind, as in Gaul, except beech and fir. Hares, fowl and geese they think it unlawful to eat, but rear them for pleasure and amusement. The climate is more temperate than in Gaul, the cold being less severe...
>
> "By far the most civilised are those living in Kent (a purely maritime district), whose way of life differs little from that of the Gauls. Most of the tribes in the interior do not grow corn but live on milk and meat, and wear skins. All the Britons dye their bodies with woad, which produces a blue colour, and this gives them a more terrifying appearance in battle. They wear their hair long and shave the whole of their bodies except the head and the upper lip."

In his first expedition in 55 B.C. Caesar brought a relatively small force for a fortnight and reached no further than the neighbourhood of Canterbury. In 54 B.C. he committed more than half of his entire operational strength. The Britons placed themselves under the command of Cassivellaunus, chief of a tribe beyond the Thames. Seven tribes are named as part of these troops, and it may well be that some of them lived near Dunstable on Puddlehill.

Caesar forced his way across the Thames, and Cassivellaunus fell back northward with 4,000 charioteers along a road, burning the crops and driving cattle into the woods. The route must surely be along the western bank of the Lea, by Cheshunt, Hertford and Hatfield, the only area where Iron Age relics

Fig. 26. Bronze Mirror found at Old Warden (Scale 1:3). Now in Bedford Museum.

have been discovered. Caesar pursued him until he captured his capital. Sir Mortimer Wheeler believed this capital was at the "Devils Dyke" in Wheathampstead, where he dug in the 1930s. This huge ditch, 40 m across and 12 m deep, is one of a number of similar massive earthworks dug near tribal capitals in south-east Britain at this time. There is another known as "Beech Bottom" on the outskirts of St. Albans.

Ravensburgh, near Hexton, has also been suggested as a possible site for the British stronghold. Caesar tells us that as the Romans stormed the defences the Britons withdrew across the opposite side. From his retreat Cassivellaunus, after an abortive diversion, offered a nominal submission, which Caesar was glad to accept, since it was already mid-September and he had to be back in Gaul before the autumn gales.

Caesar got his men safely home to face and subdue a long, bitter revolt of the Gauls, and then to make himself absolute master of the Roman world, defeating Pompey with the veterans of Gaul and Britain. It was almost a hundred years before Roman troops again set foot in Britain. It was a century

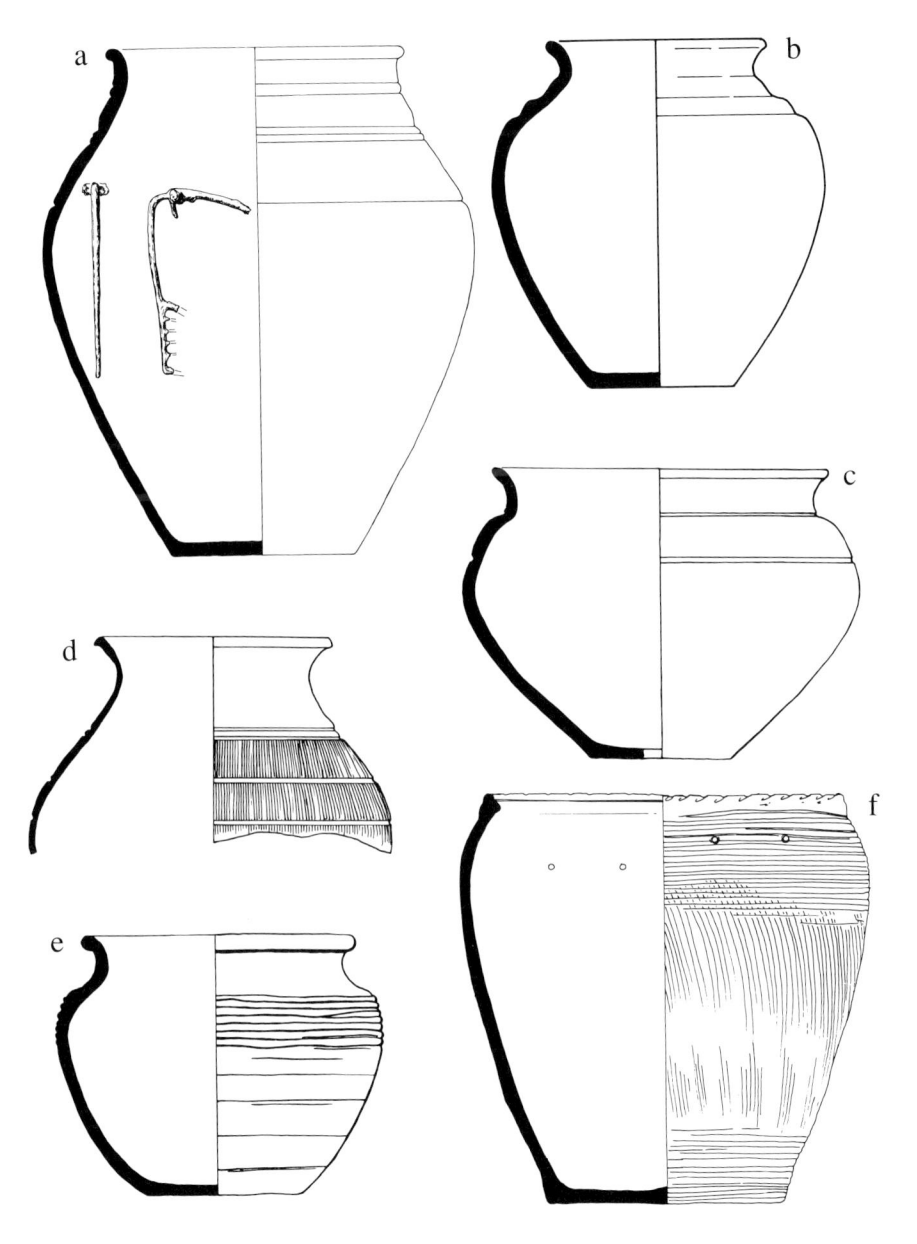

Fig. 27. Pottery of the late Pre-Roman Iron Age (sometimes called "Belgic") from Puddlehill (Scale 1:4). *a* and *b*, from a cremation.

of great change, and a good deal is known of it, although most of our evidence is the pottery and coins found in a thousand sites like Puddlehill.

Tribes and Chieftains

Caesar wrote of tribes and chieftains, and in Hertfordshire and Essex richly furnished burials have been found, dating to the century after his raids on Britain. The leaders of the time were importing wine and other luxury goods from the continent and their own craftsmen were creating high-quality metalwork, such as the iron "fire-dogs" found in chieftain burials at Welwyn and Baldock in Hertfordshire and Stanfordbury in Bedfordshire, and the beautifully decorated bronze mirrors, like the one found at Old Warden.

We know that in the Roman period the tribe whose centre was at Verulamium, the city on Watling Street near the modern St. Albans, were known as the Catuvellauni. Caesar's adversary Cassivellaunus was probably a chief of this tribe, and his successor from about 20 B.C. to about 10 A.D. was Tasciovanus, who struck coins at Verulamium, bearing his name and the name of the town. The letters inscribed on these coins are the earliest words written in Britain. Pieces of the clay moulds used to form these coins have been found at the site of his mint, near where the forum of the Roman city later stood.

Tasciovanus extended his kingdom to include parts of Suffolk, Essex and Kent. His successor, Cunobelinus, (about 10–40 A.D.), whom Shakespeare knew as Cymbeline, made himself master of all southern and central Britain, from Northampton to Southampton and from Gloucester to Colchester. He moved his capital from Verulamium to Colchester (Camulodunum).

New Settlers on Puddlehill

The final phase of pre-Roman farming activity on Puddlehill dates roughly to this century between Caesar's raids on Britain and the Roman conquest in 43 A.D. The end of the previous chapter recorded a period when no-one was living on the hill. When settlers again appear, their way of life has changed a good deal: there are no more storage pits or enclosures, the dead are cremated and buried in urns, coins are in use and the pottery is of a completely new kind.

Some archaeologists have linked the new pottery style with the Belgic immigrants described by Caesar, and therefore call it "Belgic". Another name for this culture, which avoids identification with the Belgae, is "late pre-Roman Iron Age".

The pottery was made professionally and thrown on a wheel, whereas all the earlier pottery had been made by hand. This new technique was certainly introduced from abroad. Formerly the domestic skills of cooking, sewing and making pots had been learned at home. Henceforth for 500 years the pots were the work of professionals, who made them for sale. The new potter brought not only the wheel to throw the pots, but new firing techniques, and so was able to produce much harder pots of entirely new shapes, different from those of the earlier Iron Age people. They appear in south-east Britain in the first century B.C. and spread as far as Bedfordshire and Northamptonshire. It is hard to date this pottery precisely. We can only be sure of the time when it was used whereit is found together with Roman pottery. The Roman armies occupied Germany between the Rhine and Elbe for a quarter of a century, between 15 B.C. and 9 A.D. In that area several forts have been excavated, and in them was found a great deal of Roman and Belgic pottery which must have been in use within these years. In Britain much of this kind of pottery is believed to be earlier, since it lacks certain distinctive pot shapes introduced about 15 B.C.

This high quality pottery, new to Britain, was certainly in widespread use in our area in the century before the Roman conquest, but we must not assume that the people using it were necessarily foreign immigrants: the ownership of a Japanese camera or motor bike does not make someone Japanese.

In the previous chapter we noted that hand-made imitations of the new pot styles were found among the middle Iron Age wares on Puddlehill. It looks as though, if there were indeed new people in the area, the first contact with the earlier population was one of peaceful co-operation and the local people copied the strangers' pots. Later, the old way of life, along with the hand-made pottery, was completely swept away.

The earliest levels of the new occupation are found in the semi-silted Iron Age ditches. Here, in the hollows sheltered from the wind, they built their cooking hearths and scattered the animal meal bones around them. Unlike the earlier peoples, who deposited their refuse in abandoned storage pits, these late Iron Age people built hearth upon hearth and sat upon the bones of previous meals until the debris in some ditch hollows was 75 cm thick.

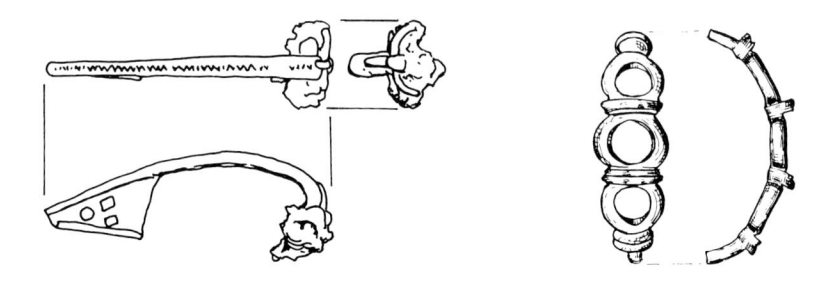

Fig. 28. Bronze objects of the late Iron Age from Puddlehill. A Brooch and a Tankard Handle (Scale 1:2).

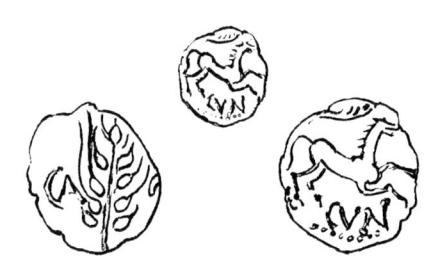

Fig. 29. Coin of Cunobelinus (10–40 A.D.) found in Leagrave. Actual size and enlarged. It is inscribed CVN for Cunobelinus and CA for Camulodunum (Colchester) his capital.

Although these people must have been living and working on Puddlehill for many years it is impossible to trace change or development in this mass-produced pottery. There were variations on a number of standard shapes, most of which were found at all levels of the occupation (Fig. 27). When ornamentation was used they favoured combed decoration and cordons below the neck of the vessel. The fabric of the pot was well-fired and hard. Often the clay was tempered with crushed shell, giving the surface a "soapy" feel.

Many of these pots had holes pierced in the base long after the clay had been fired. What they were used for we do not know: certainly not colanders; when they wanted this type of vessel the holes were pierced before the pot was fired. The number of holes in the pots varied from as many as nine to a single large hole in the bottom, and in one case the pot so drilled had burnt "porridge" on the inside, and in another the pot had broken during the drilling of the holes. The pots with these holes were being put to a secondary use, probably after they had become too soured for cooking purposes. Perhaps they were used as flower pots to grow special kinds of herbs. A whole mass of Field Gromwell seed was found near one house.

Where the earlier farmers had lived in well-constructed communal dwellings built perhaps to house thirty people, the late Iron Age people lived in small one-roomed huts or perhaps skin wigwams big enough for one couple with their children. One hut site that we have found was a circular pit dug one metre deep into the chalk. Around the pit they had left a baulk of chalk to provide what may have been seating accommodation.

Perhaps they only used their hill as pasture for flocks and herds during the summer, and the hearths that we find are the summer residents' cooking places. They left many meal bones amongst their rubbish, and beef bones outnumber mutton and pork.

One more permanent kind of hut showed as a circle of postholes over one of the Iron Age ditches. This belonged to the period around the time of the Roman invasion of 43 A.D.

Although Caesar says the common British people of his time were little better than slaves, some of the wealth displayed in the chieftain burials trickled down to the Puddlehill farmers: for the first time decorative metalwork appears amongst the refuse. A fine tankard handle (Fig. 28), several brooches, a needle and simple tweezers, all of bronze, belong to the first century A.D. There were also two silver coins of Cunobelinus, chief of the Catuvellauni between 10 A.D. and 40 A.D.

Cremation

Sir Mortimer Wheeler carried out excavations at Prae Wood, west of the Roman city of Verulamium, and he found an extensive settlement of the late "Belgic" period. This was probably the tribal capital of the Catuvellauni, which was moved down on to the Watling Street after the Roman conquest and reconstructed as a Roman-style city. Not far from Prae Wood and just to the west of the Roman city wall is a large cremation cemetery which spans the period from about 1 A.D. to 60 A.D.

This new rite of cremation was also in use on Puddlehill. The funeral practices of the earlier Iron Age peoples are unknown to us – burials are rarely found – but in the last century before the Roman conquest cemeteries of cremated bones buried in the new-style pots became widespread in the south and east of Britain. A group of nine cremations was found on Puddlehill.

In the semi-silted ditch of Enclosure I a grave was dug and a dead person placed in it. A fire of oak timbers was lit above the body, which was consumed totally by the intense heat. Debris which had been emptied out of the ditch when the grave was dug and thrown back after the cremation included animal bones left by previous people. Scorch marks on these bones where they came in contact with the embers of the fireshow that the grave had been filled in whilst the ashes were still hot. Perhaps wealthier people received more attention. Sometimes the ashes of the person cremated were collected and placed in an urn which was buried in a hole in the chalk. Fig. 27 shows such a burial urn. This contained burnt bones and a burnt iron brooch that once fastened the person's cloak. A smaller pot with the burial was found empty and had probably contained some form of wine or mead for the deceased's last journey. Sometimes the ashes are found in shallow holes dug into the chalk. They had probably originally been placed in a basket or bag.

Ditch Systems

Down the slope of the hill towards Houghton Regis, some distance from the cemetery and from the Iron Age farmsteads, was a puzzling network of shallow ditches containing broken pottery and other debris of the late Iron Age period. They were not boundaries or enclosures, nor were they required for drainage on this dry chalk hillside. They seemed designed, though rather haphazardly, to collect rain water and direct it into hollowed-out basins in the chalk. Very similar gullies and basins of similar date have also been found on the hillside on the west of Watling Street, above Sewell Lane. It has been suggested that they were used in some industrial process such as tanning, or the treatment of cloth.

The whole area of Dunstable became fairly thickly populated during this period. Ditches containing late Iron Age pottery have been found during building or road-making operations on the Brewers Hill estate, at Beecroft, Southfields, Lowther Road, Ardley Hill and Skimpot.

The End of British Independence

Whilst these changes were taking place in Britain during the century after Caesar, even greater changes were taking place in Rome. Caesar was assassinated in 44 B.C. when he was at the height of his power. After thirteen years of civil war, his adopted son Augustus made himself sole ruler and established an imperial monarchy that lasted for many centuries. Its most striking achievement was peace. For 250 years, though campaigns were fought on the frontiers, the only armed conflicts within the frontiers were two short and local civil wars, involving few but the regular army. Most of western and central Europe and all the lands that border the Mediterranean, have known no such unbroken peace since then. Augustus and his successor, Tiberius, ruled for seventy years between them. Their aim was peaceful consolidation. Gaul became thoroughly Roman, a land of Roman cities whose elected magistrates bore Roman names, spoke Latin and thought Roman. In Britain princes and nobles bought foreign luxury imports; but this scarcely affected their subjects.

In the excavations of Colchester and Verulamium were very many imported pots, together with the native wares. On Puddlehill and other local sites are the same native wares, some local copies of the imports but only very few actual continental pots. Britain stayed as it was because Augustus and Tiberius refused to risk military adventures abroad.

Tiberius died in 37 A.D., and the British ruler Cunobelinus in 40 A.D. Tiberius was succeeded by Caligula, who planned a conquest of Britain but was murdered in January 41 A.D. His successor, Claudius, carried out the invasion in 43 A.D. A large Roman army of 40,000 men, in four legions of around five thousand men apiece, backed by some thirty or forty independent battalions or auxiliary cohorts, invaded Britain. The campaign was quickly over, and in two months Cunobelinus' son, Caratacus, was beaten, Colchester taken and his kingdom annexed. Though he resisted in the highlands of Wales, the conquest of the main kingdom was complete. The Roman armies pushed out at once to the frontiers of Cunobelinus' realm, and the Dunstable region became Roman.

CHAPTER VII

The Roman Period

The Effect of the Roman Conquest on Puddlehill

On Puddlehill the consequences of the Roman invasion were immediate and dramatic. The hut of the native farmers was destroyed; in their ditches, two oxen were roasted whole and only partly eaten. Their pottery was smashed. Some pieces of pottery found in the ashes of the fire that roasted the oxen belonged to pots lying broken on the floor of the hut. The pottery dates to within a few years of the Roman invasion. The plunderers might have been Roman soldiers or they might have been brigands who took advantage of the troubled times; but their raid was clearly a consequence of the conquest.

The Roman impact on the farmers of Puddlehill must have been shattering: within a short time of the successful invasion the conquerors began to drive military roads through the British countryside. One of the most important, linking London to Chester and North Wales, was Watling Street, cutting straight across the top of Puddlehill.

The roads were probably built by forced labour under the supervision of Imperial troops. Where the Watling Street crossed the highest point of Puddlehill, evidence was found of a large beacon fire. A saucer-shaped depression some 4 m across and 50 cm deep had been dug into the chalk to contain a large and very hot fire over a short period. Within the ashes of the fire were found forged iron nails, showing that some dressed timbers had been used to feed the flames. A fragment of an early black Roman dish was found on the virgin chalk away from the fire. Other fragments of the same pot were found burnt brick red in the ashes. Other pottery fragments found included a mica-dusted vessel decorated with circles that was probably a pot made by a legionary potter. This may or may not have been the camp site of the Roman Legions who marched along the Watling Street, but it certainly belongs to the earliest Roman period, and almost certainly some of the farmers' buildings went into the fire. Beacons were probably used to sight from one hilltop to the next when laying out the alignment of a Roman road.

The future of Puddlehill after this Roman conquest was less dramatic; all that survived are a few separate little clusters of pottery, most of them of the early Roman period, and foundations of primitive buildings and work places. It may well be that the Roman farm moved to the sheltered slope on the southern side of the hill. The quarrymen reported that before excavation of the site began they had quarried away the flint foundations of a substantial building and had found pottery decorated with hunting scenes. The structures on the hilltop may have been the remnants of outbuildings or peasants' quarters.

An innovation to British agriculture at this time was the corn-drying kiln (Plate 9). Two were found on the hilltop and they consisted of a flue and a floor built on columns for drying grain, and perhaps also for malting barley to make beer. These kilns were peculiar to Britain and many have been found, usually datable to the third or fourth century A.D., but on Puddlehill when they went out of use they were filled with rubbish that included pottery, none of it much later than the reign of Claudius. It is evident that in Britain this simple type of corn-drying kiln came into use soon after the conquest. Under the collapsed roof of the flue we found a mass of eggshells. A farmyard hen had used the abandoned kiln as a nesting place before it had been destroyed and filled in with rubbish.

The walls of the huts or barns were found as shallow ditches dug to contain wooden sleeper-beams into which wooden uprights were apparently set. One of the beams had been made from a large tree trunk and the trench to contain it still followed the shape of the tree; wide at the base and narrower at the top. The spaces between the uprights would be filled with wattle and daubed with clay. Some of this clay survived alongside the sleeper trenches.

The floor of the building was hard packed earth and in this we found

Plate 9. Roman corn-drying kiln under excavation, Puddlehill.

several broken brooches and one complete little brooch made from a single strip of bronze.

Several iron rings and knives were found on the floor. The knives included two pruning knives where the blade is turned 125 degrees to the socket. Other fragments of iron may be pieces of ploughshares. Several of the farmer's boots were found. The leather or wood had long disappeared, but the iron hob nails were still lying in the pattern of the boots' soles and heels. In one, a small iron bar had been inserted across the instep.

Dog skeletons were numerous. One of them had had all the back teeth removed during its lifetime. This had been done to give it a "soft mouth"; the dog had obviously been used as a retriever. An interesting little episode concerning dogs was discovered during the excavations. Within a silted ditch, buried during this Roman period, we found the skeleton of a dog minus a tail. A little further on another dog was found with the front right paw missing completely; the back right paw was twisted back beneath the dog; obviously it had only been hanging on by a sinew. We then found a dog's skull which had been severed from the body by a clean blow, and later discovered what was probably the reason for this slaughter of dogs: a complete sheep skeleton. This had been buried while rigor mortis was in the body. Although it was lying on its side it had died in a kneeling position with its head between its front legs. Beyond the skeleton of the sheep was the carcase of the dog with the head missing. We do not really know the story behind this, but it does look as though the dogs had been guilty of sheep worrying and the farmer in his rage had sliced off the head of one dog with a swordlike weapon and had made a wild swing at another, cutting off the front paw and almost slicing off the back paw. The sheep, probably brought in by a slave from the downs, must have been too badly mauled to have been used in the stew pot.

The only Roman coin found within this area was a small bronze of Nero (54–68 A.D.). Coinage in this early period was still rather scarce although pots were now being bought in the market. The pottery found on Puddlehill contains a few fragments of fine red ware known as "Terra Sigillata" or "Samian". This was being imported from Gaulish potteries by the shipload; but British potteries were now becoming active and the local products included flagons and mixing bowls called "mortaria" made with a creamy white fabric. The imported Samian and mortaria were often stamped with the potter's name, and the local potter often imitated this stamping. Within the hut we found a fragment of Mortarium that carried one of these local cypher stamps. The potter had been unable to spell correctly, and had therefore jumbled the letters together into an incoherent tangle. The form and fabric of this vessel suggest that it was made between 100 and 150 A.D., probably nearer 100 than later.

Roman Roads and Towns

The Roman conquest meant a great deal more than isolated farmsteads and the bric-a-brac of their civilization. In all Roman provinces, the armies guarded the frontiers, while Rome ruled the interior through the native chieftains with the least possible cost and effort to the Roman Government. The Government generously financed the initial capital outlay on founding a new province, and thereafter ran it at the least possible annual cost. The Romans built wide straight roads to connect the frontier armies with one another and with the army headquarters. Along the roads they maintained a regular service of mounted couriers, fast passenger carriages and heavy goods wagons for government business; and they established a series of remounting stages anywhere from eight to fifteen miles apart, with a larger establishment with overnight accommodation at every second or third stage.

In Britain the main roads radiated from London. There were six of them, the main trunk roads to Colchester, Canterbury, Chichester, Staines and the West, to Chester and to York. Verulamium (the city of the Catuvellauni) and Dunstable (Durocobrivis) lay upon the Chester Road – the Watling Street.

After the making of the Watling Street the history of Dunstable turns upon the crossing of the Icknield Way (which had existed as a routeway since Neolithic times) and the Roman road – the modern crossroads. The roads were the main ancient routes of Britain, and in terms of road communications, Dunstable was the centre of England.

The crossing of the two important roads was a convenient distance – just twelve Roman miles – from Verulamium, for it to become a stopping place on long journeys. It was almost certainly a staging post on the Government communication network, with horses kept in readiness for messengers on official business. Travellers in less of a hurry could stop for a meal or even stay overnight.

The Romans used their larger staging points for an additional purpose – to make sure that loyal native leaders governed the provinces efficiently and safely. They induced the chiefs of each tribe to adopt Roman ways and live in a town laid out by Roman surveyors, with a town centre, a town hall, public baths, usually a theatre or amphitheatre, and other public buildings and private houses.

Each civitas or tribe was equipped with such a city; the chiefs became men of property, living on rents from their peasants, spending their income on a town house and town goods, elected as councillors and magistrates – a smaller version of Rome itself.

Once their property consisted of good, permanent houses located in a town, there was little fear of rebellion. The property and interest of the notables was fixed and immovable, and easily at the control of the Government. With their natural native leaders firmly tied to the interest of the Government, there was little fear of rebellion by leaderless peasants.

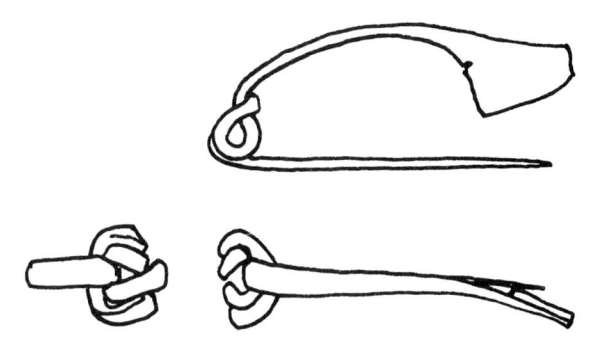

Fig. 30. Bronze brooch from Puddlehill (Actual size).

All such towns are sited on the main roads. The town of the Catuvellauni was built along the Watling Street at St. Albans, on low ground beneath the ancient fortress of Tasciovanus – still called by the ancient name of Verulamium. This was the political and social capital of the Dunstable region for four centuries.

Much is known of Verulamium. When the first edition of this book was published in 1963 the writer stated that "very little" was known of Roman Dunstable, named on Roman road maps "Durocobrivis" (sometimes interpreted as "Durocobrivae"). There was even some doubt as to whether the Roman town had been on the same site as the modern one. In the ten years which followed, however, the redevelopment of the town centre began, and the quantity of Roman material which came to light on many sites in the town left no doubt that we had found Durocobrivis.

Some staging towns grew up on the site of a fort built by troops in the conquest period; such was the origin of Towcester (Lactodorum). There was a fort at Magiovinium, the next town along the road to the north of Durocobrivis, and at Verulamium itself. We might expect a small fortification in Durocobrivis as well. No evidence of any defences has yet been found here, nor anything to indicate the presence of the army.

The Boudican Revolt

If there was a town here in the early years after the Roman conquest it must have been razed to the ground during the Boudican revolt. The King of the Iceni, a tribe occupying the area of Norfolk, died and in his will named the Emperor Nero as co-heir with his two daughters. In this way he hoped to preserve his kingdom, but the writer Tacitus says: "Kingdom and household were plundered like prizes of war, the one by Roman officers, the other by Roman slaves. As a beginning, his widow, Boudica, was flogged, and their daughters raped. The Icenian chiefs were deprived of their hereditary estates as if the Romans had been given the whole country. The King's own relatives were treated like slaves."

This avarice, condemned by the Roman writer Tacitus, led to one of the bloodiest episodes in the history of Britain. In 61 A.D. the Iceni revolted and descended in hordes on the great Roman city of Colchester, burning and massacring the hated Romans. From Colchester they marched to London and Verulamium. All who had not fled were killed, their homes looted and burnt. Tacitus says that Roman and provincial deaths numbered 70,000. Archaeology confirms this story. Excavations at Verulamium show a deep layer of ash at the level of the earliest Roman city. A Roman Dunstable would have suffered the same fate at this time. The revolt was put down only after London had been sacked, and the victorious Iceni marching northwards along the Watling Street met the trained Roman army brought down from north Wales. The red-haired Boudica poisoned herself and a terrible vengeance was taken by the Roman army on her tribe. This was the last serious opposition to the Roman occupation in the south. Verulamium was

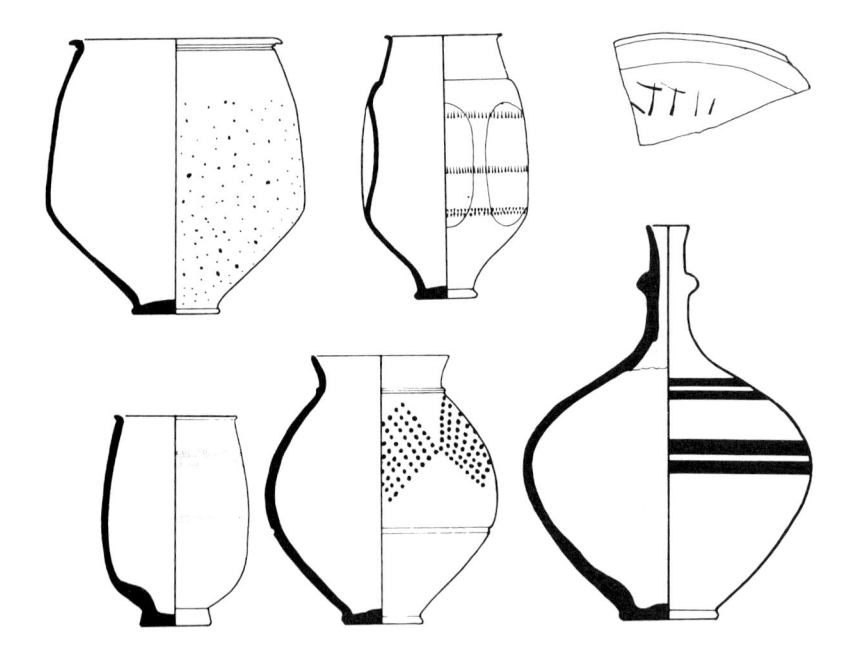

Fig. 31. Pottery from Roman Dunstable (Scale 1:4).

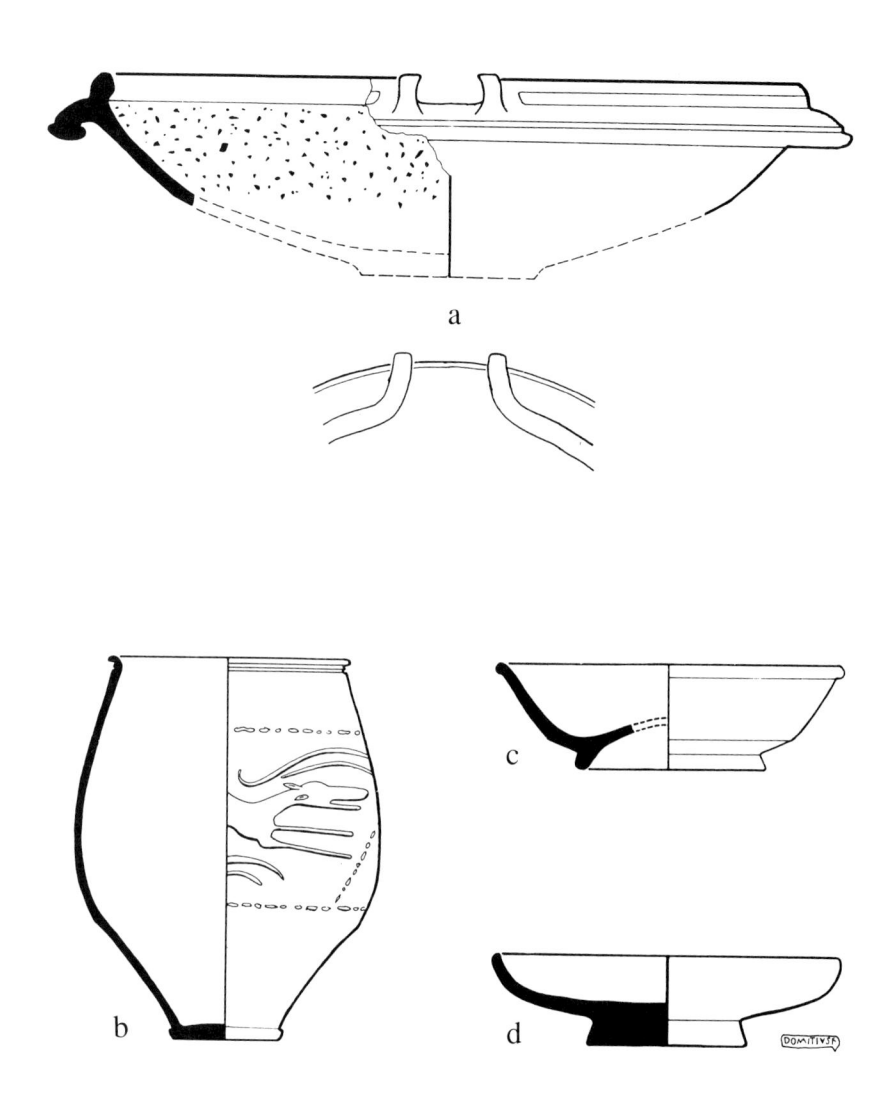

Fig. 31 continued.
a   A mortarium. These were used for grinding up food with a pestle and had stone grits embedded in the inner surface to make it rougher and less likely to wear away.
b   A cup decorated with a hunting scene of dogs chasing a stag.
c, d   Imported Samian vessels. One has the stamp DOMITIUS F inside the base.

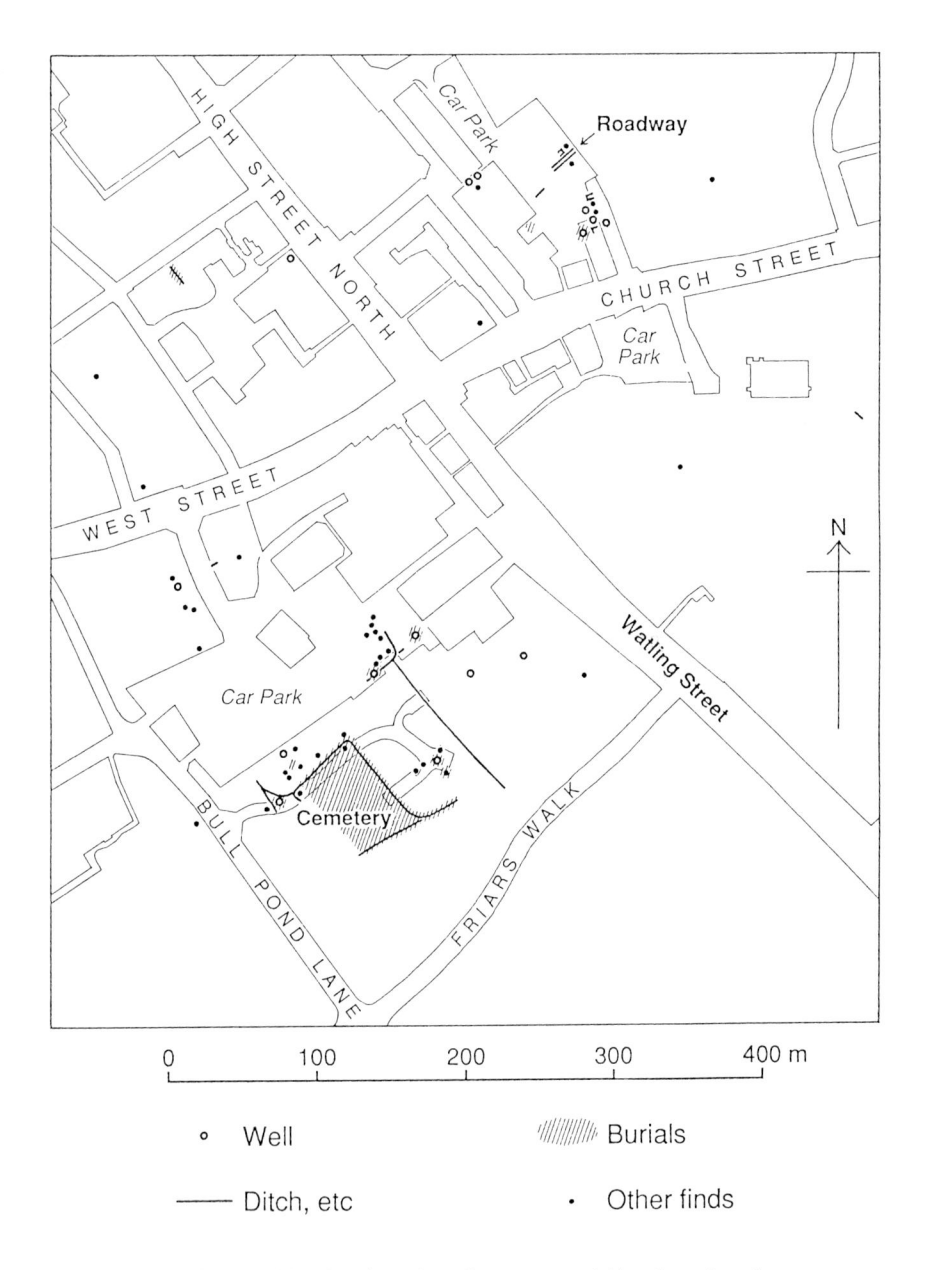

Fig. 32. Plan of Dunstable, showing where Roman material has been found.

rebuilt, and undoubtedly Roman Dunstable, and the great peace – the Pax Britannica – had begun.

The Romano-British Town of Durocobrivis

We talk of the period in Britain from 43 A.D. to about 400 A.D. as "Roman", but it should be emphasised that the population of the country remained British – the descendants of the people who had lived here since prehistoric times. The impact of the conquerors on the way of life, particularly in the towns, was strong, and as the centuries passed Britain became increasingly Romanised. We therefore often use the term "Romano-British" to describe the people and the culture of the period when Britain was part of the Empire.

Durocobrivis may have been a centre of local government with a local British landowner (perhaps the occupier of the great villa at Totternhoe) acting as magistrate and deputy to the main tribal administration in Verulamium. Certainly it must have become a market town, attracting local farmers, traders and craftsmen to sell to passing travellers and to buy, in turn, mass-produced or imported goods such as pottery, glass and metalwork.

The earliest buildings of the Roman settlement will have been along the new road, which is now the High Street of Dunstable. The later houses and shops of the medieval and modern town, most of them with cellars dug into the chalk, must have destroyed the evidence for what stood there in the first century A.D. The excavations that have been possible in the last twenty five years have all been set back from the central street crossing in areas which became occupied as Durocobrivis expanded in the second century and later.

All through its history, Dunstable has owed its existence to the Watling Street and its crossing with the Icknield Way. In the days of the stage coach, inns sprang up all along the route, and even today the number of eating-places of every nationality in the town centre is far above the needs of the native population. It must have been the same in Roman times, with inns to serve travellers, and blacksmiths, wheelwrights and corn merchants providing the sort of service we look for today at a garage.

Only one metalled road of the Roman period has been uncovered in the town. This lies under the Quadrant car park and runs parallel to Church Street. It may have been the route taken at that time by the Icknield Way, or, as it was not very wide, nor kept very clean, perhaps it was a back street. The ruts were cobbled with pebbles, but over the years the track became deep in mud and rubbish and from time to time a rubble of stones and tiles was dumped on it to fill the potholes. Fourteen coins had been lost in the mud and rubbish over a length of about 8 m, the earliest of Marcus Aurelius (161–180 A.D.) and the latest the House of Constantine, c.340 A.D. There were also iron keys, much pottery and other household rubbish, and an ox-shoe. These "hippo sandals" were tied on to the hooves of animals when they had to travel on hard-surfaced roads.

Evidence of the Romano-British town has been found in all four quadrants of Dunstable and seems to cover a wider area than that of the medieval town. In the south west quadrant, where there has been the best opportunity to excavate, Romano-British features have been found reaching as far west from Watling Street as Bull Pond Lane and as far south as Friars Walk, and they may go further.

The finds suggest expansion in the second century to form a thriving town, which lasted, with varying fortunes, at least to the end of the fourth century.

No evidence has yet appeared of substantial or well-to-do houses. If such there were, they must have been along the main road and their remains obliterated by later building. We have found no stone walls or under-floor heating (hypocausts) and very little building brick, which suggests that the houses, stables etc. were constructed of wood. Most of them were probably thatched, but some were tiled in the distinctive Roman manner (see Fig 33). So far, not even a single little square tessera from a mosaic or tessellated floor has been identified in Dunstable: it was a town not of elegant apartments and togas but of simple accommodation and hob-nailed boots.

There is one other Roman town known in Bedfordshire: at Sandy, on the Ermine Street, and the finds of metalwork, jewellery and so on there suggest a higher standard of living than that at Durocobrivis.

Another settlement of the period, not substantial enough to be called a town, but covering quite a large area, was at Limbury on the Icknield Way

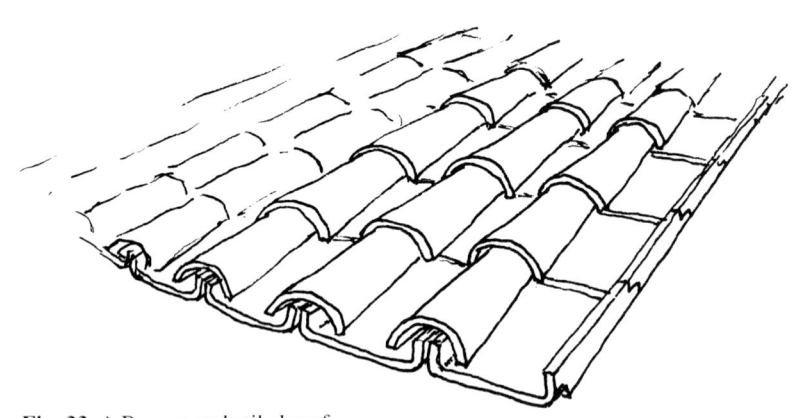

Fig. 33. A Roman-style tiled roof.

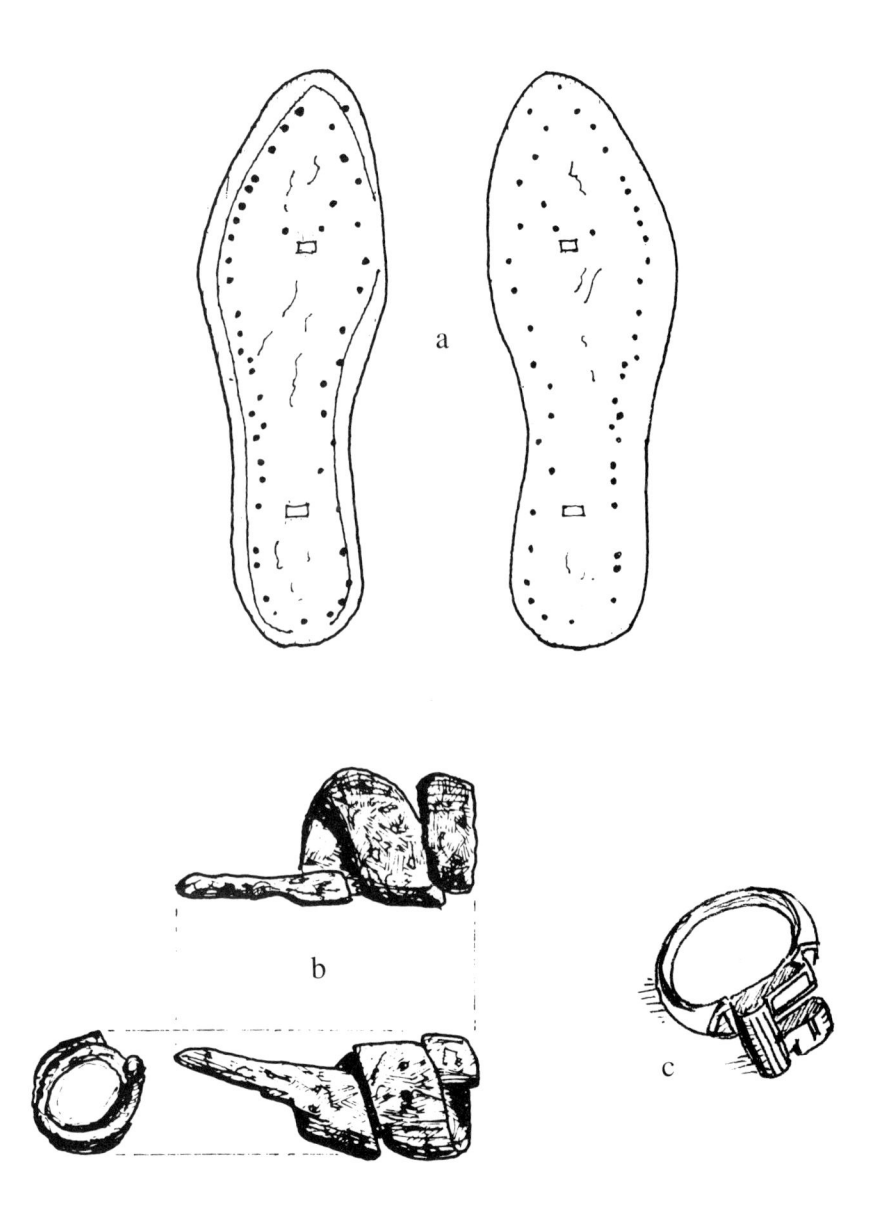

Fig. 34. Finds from a Roman well in Dunstable
a   Insole from a shoe, drawn from both sides (Scale 1:3)
b   Ox-goad (Actual size)
c   Silver Ring with Key (Actual size)

north of Luton, where much Roman material has been found during the construction of new roads and houses.

Life in Roman Dunstable

The greater part of the finds from Roman Dunstable come not from the sites of houses but from pits, ditches and wells. The total absence of natural surface water meant that the inhabitants had to dig down through the chalk to a depth of about 30 m for their water supply. Nineteen Roman wells have been located in Dunstable, but only one has so far been completely excavated by archaeologists. Its chalk walls were unlined and had footholds scooped out on opposite sides at intervals of 38 cm so that the well diggers could climb up and down. It had been dug in the second century and had been in use for many years. Then it had been filled in with chalk and rubbish. As we emptied this out again we found that the bottom of the well filled with water to a depth of nearly 10 m, showing that the water table is higher in this area today than it was in the second century A.D. The archaeologists had to use skin diving equipment to reach the bottom.

Wet conditions preserve organic materials like wood and leather, and

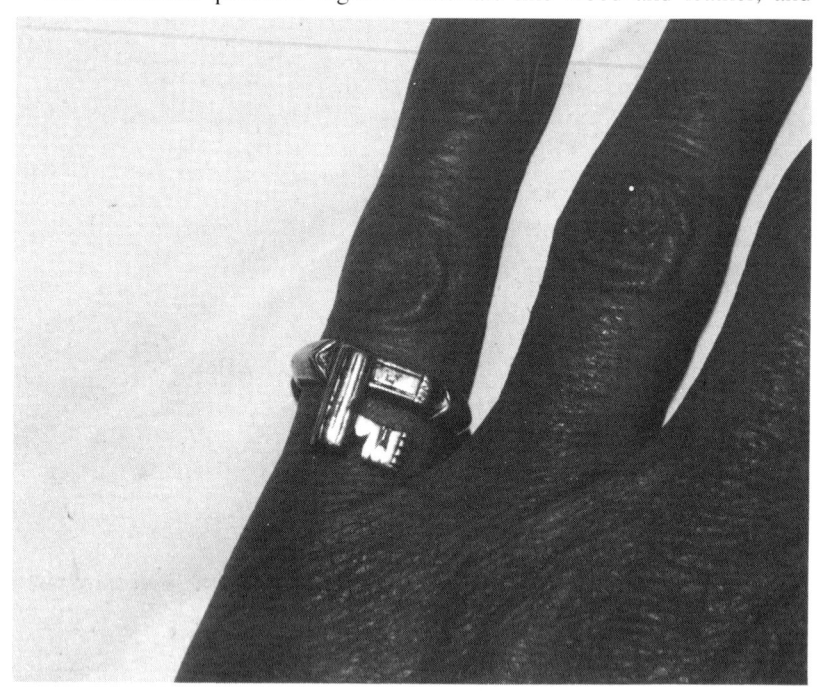

Plate 10. Silver Ring found in a Roman well in Dunstable.

among the objects found lying at the bottom of the well were the sole of a shoe and the staves of a wooden bucket, bound with iron bands. There was also a silver finger ring with a key (Fig. 34 and Plate 10). It is difficult to imagine this being dropped by accident into the well: we can speculate as to why it was there. Was it cast in with a wish, a vow, or after a disappointment in love? Such personal items as jewellery or the shoe bring us closer for a moment to the real people who lived in Roman Dunstable.

In the area which is now a car park behind the shops (Sainsbury's etc.) in the south-west quadrant of the town were two more wells and a number of rubbish pits. These were presumably in the back yards of the Roman-period roadside premises. For the archaeologists they were a rich source of information about the life of the time. The remains of food included, as well as bones from beef, mutton, pork and chicken, the shells of oyster, and also a few whelks, mussels and scallops. These must have been brought in barrels from the coast. Oysters remained a cheap food into Victorian times and their shells are common on sites of many periods, even so far from the sea as Bedfordshire.

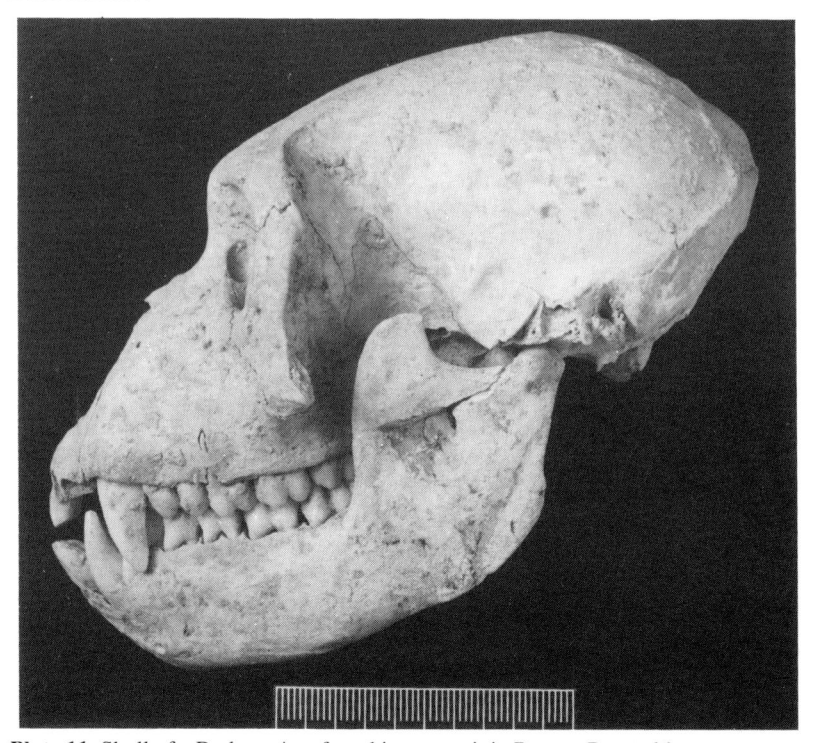

Plate 11. Skull of a Barbary Ape found in a cesspit in Roman Dunstable.

Another shell that was found deep in a second century pit was that of a garden snail. This may not sound remarkable, but it is believed that this species (*Helix aspersa*) was first introduced to Britain by the Romans in the first century A.D. for eating, so this one was an early predecessor of those in our gardens today. Worthington Smith reported a pile of shells of this species found with Roman pottery in Totternhoe. This period also saw the introduction of the larger Edible or Roman Snail (*H. pomatia*) but this has not been found in Roman Dunstable.

Not all the animal remains from rubbish pits were from food species. Horse bones form a large proportion (though these may have contributed to the diet as well as being working animals). Cats and dogs were kept in the town and a much more unusual pet also found his last resting place in a second century pit. This was a young Barbary Ape, the species familiar on Gibraltar and popular with the Romans as a pet, coming originally from North Africa. The Dunstable ape had just reached the age when his teeth and his temper might have become dangerous and caused his life to be cut short; or perhaps Dunstable's sharp winter was too much for his tender southern constitution. Imagination must be called in to reconstruct the story of who brought him here and why.

Another unexpected presence in Bedfordshire was a White-Tailed Sea Eagle, a bird bigger than the Golden Eagle, which was a native of Britain up till the nineteenth century but which normally frequents coasts. Near where its bones lay in a deep rubbish pit were the skeletons of a frog and a water vole, which may have been its last meal.

As on so many archaeological sites a large proportion of the finds consisted of pottery. It was all mass-produced in workshops. No kiln has been identified nearer to Dunstable than the St. Albans area, where many everyday household wares were produced. Distinctive styles of pot found here came from Oxford, the Nene Valley near Peterborough, and other production centres. Some quality wares, especially the glossy red Samian pots, were imported from Gaul, and high-quality glass bottles, bowls and drinking glasses came from the Rhineland. Many different shapes of ceramic vessels were fairly standardised across large areas of the Empire, though with local variations, and a great variety of them has been found in Dunstable (see Fig. 31 for some examples). Large jars called "amphorae" were imported to Britain in large numbers as containers for wine, olive oil and fish sauce, but not many have been found in Durocobrivis. This suggests that there was little market for these luxury items here, nor, it seems, for clay lamps: none have been found here, despite being a relatively common item elsewhere.

Craftsmen's tools that have been found include a large two-pronged iron rake, with fragments of the wooden handle still in its socket, and a file and a rasp found together with the lynch-pin from a cartwheel. These appeared to have been wrapped in cloth and dropped in the bottom of the pit where the Sea Eagle was found. The many small articles of iron and bronze which have been found are too numerous to list here, but one type of which there were several examples was an ox-goad (Fig. 34): these were fixed to the end of a pole and used to prod draft animals into livelier action. They were also found on Puddlehill.

There is evidence that metal-working was carried on in the outskirts of the town, although of course the raw materials were not available locally. Lumps of iron slag show that smiths were working and their hearths have also been found. A small bronze worker's furnace was identified by finding fragments and droplets of the metal mixed with layers of ash.

Burials

For the first century or more after the Roman Conquest cremation continued as the usual funeral custom, but then the fashion began to change and in the later Roman period burial in a grave (inhumation) became general. Under Roman law cemeteries were not permitted inside towns and they usually lay beside roads leading out of settlements. Only one Romano-British cremation, in an urn, has been found in Dunstable so far: it turned up during construction work on the Quadrant shopping site. An inhumation cemetery has, however, been found in the Friary Field area, some 200 m south-west of High Street South. We can therefore assume that this was outside the inhabited area of the town. Evidence of coins and pottery for the date of these burials indicates the fourth century; some at least were late in the century or may even have been after 400 A.D. Fig. 35 is a good example of a coin providing dating evidence: the ditch surrounding the area of the burials had been allowed to silt up over the years and when 50 cm of this fill had accumulated someone lost a coin, dropping it into what was by this time only a shallow gully. The coin was one of Valens, dating to 364–378 A.D. so the loss must have occurred in 364 or later; the coin showed signs of use and wear before its loss. The build-up of soil continued (with the help of earthworms and rotting vegetation) until the coin was covered by 5 cm of earth, indicating the passage of some

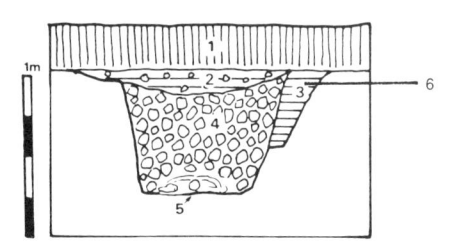

Fig. 35. Section through Cemetery Ditch and Grave.
1 Topsoil
2 Loam and chalk
3 Dark loam fill of ditch
4 Lump chalk, fill of grave
5 Skeleton
6 Depth at which coin was found

years. Then a grave was dug, cutting into the fill of the ditch near where the coin lay. This shows that the burial took place after, say, 380 A.D. and probably some years after.

Burials in the ditch (where digging was easy), rather than in graves cut into the solid chalk, were a feature of the cemetery. Fifty human skeletons were found in the ditch, along with four horses and a dog. Some of the burials cut into each other, showing that they had been made at different times. There were fifty-five graves in the area enclosed by the ditch. Other bodies had been disposed of in the area round about, in the hollows above filled-in wells and pits: more evidence of the late date of the burials. Of the Roman wells found near the cemetery five had human remains buried in the top of them.

The majority of the bodies had been laid on their backs. Iron nails showed that some had coffins. Some, however, had been tumbled into graves, where they lay sprawled or face down (Fig. 36).

Of the 112 skeletons found, five men, six women and a baby had been beheaded. This is not unusual in cemeteries of the late Romano-British period, and it seems probable that these represent not executions, but some rite carried out after death, perhaps to prevent the ghost from walking, or connected with a cult of the human head. Certainly some of the decapitated corpses had been buried carefully, with grave offerings of pots. The skull was usually placed between the legs.

One woman had her legs as well as her head chopped off (Plate 12) and a middle-aged man, whose left leg had been shortened by a fracture which had healed well many years before his death, had been buried with his right foot, cut off above the ankle, placed beside him.

The most interesting pot from the cemetery was buried with a young man. An inscription in Latin had been scratched into its surface before it was placed, already broken, next to his head (Fig. 37). The words (the only ones we have from Roman Dunstable) have been interpreted as linking the man with the "Dendrophori" or branch-bearers. These played a part in the cult of the goddess Cybele, and it is believed that the triangular temple at Verulamium was dedicated to her worship. She may also have been "patron" of a burial club, possibly for carpenters.

By the late fourth century Christianity was the official religion of the Empire, and is known to have been widespread in Britain, but no evidence has been found for it in the cemetery or elsewhere in Durocobrivis.

Three girls had their jewellery buried with them. One was wearing bracelets and rings and a string of little blue glass beads. The other two had bags or boxes containing their treasures laid beside them in the grave. The child-size bracelets of jet, bronze and gilt placed with an eight-year-old are a touching reminder of family affection and sorrow long ago.

It is often stated that people in the past were much smaller than we are

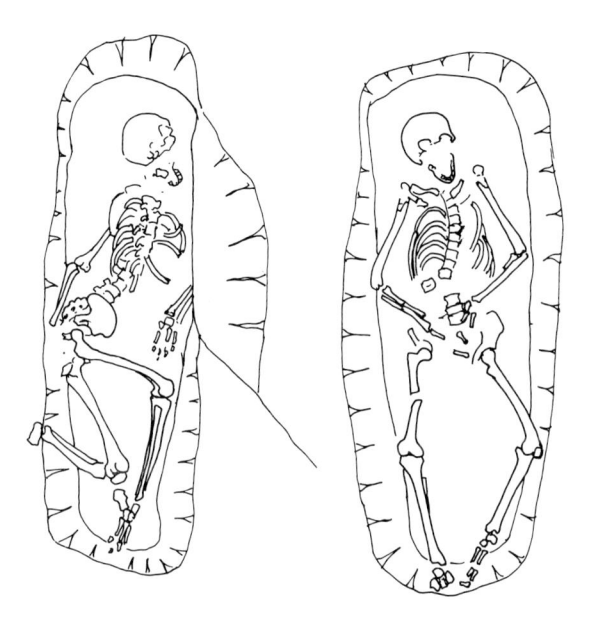

Fig. 36. Two Burials in the Dunstable Romano-British Cemetery.

today. It is therefore interesting to record the average heights of the Britons buried in Durocobrivis, calculated from the lengths of their long bones:

Men – 5 ft 7 ins (168 cm)   Women – 5 ft 3 ins (160 cm)

The average in Britain today, according to the Office of Population Censuses and Surveys, is:

Men – 5 ft 8 $^1/_2$ ins (174 cm)   Women – 5 ft 3 $^1/_2$ ins (161 cm)

The state of the teeth of the young people was good, ten of them between the ages of 20 and 30 having perfect sets, but as they grew older many teeth were lost.

There was no sign of rickets or other effects of malnutrition, but arthritis, particularly in the spine, was common.

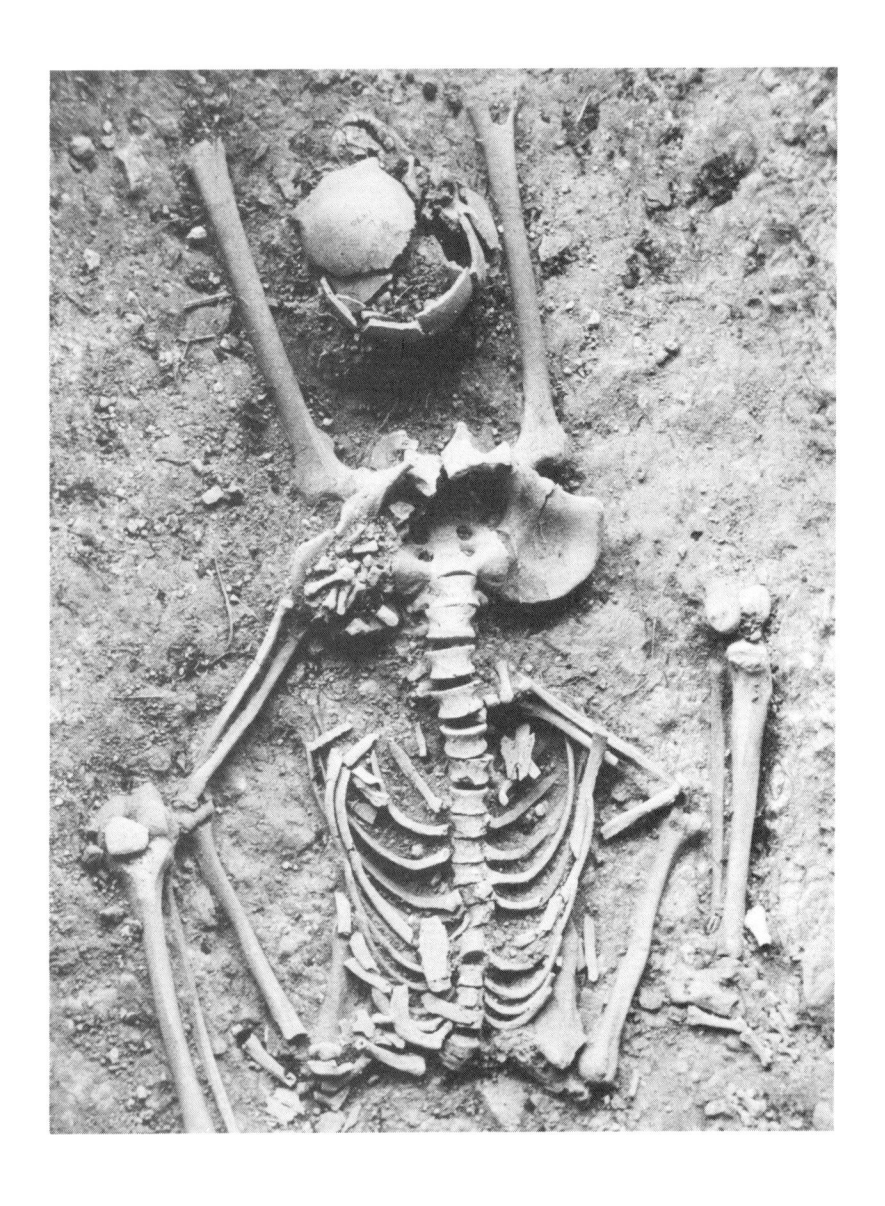

Plate 12. Mutilated Skeleton from the Romano-British cemetery in Dunstable.

Plate 13. Decapitated skeleton.

The Historical Background

For the first two centuries of Roman rule, Britain was two nations: Romans and Romanised Britons in the Latin towns, and native non-Roman peasants in the farms around. As time passed some of the farms prospered, especially those that lay near roads and towns. The little native huts were replaced by a stout farmhouse of a dozen or more rooms, built of stone or at least on foundations of stone and flint. The farms at Park Street by St. Albans and at Lockleys by the Roman town of Welwyn, developed in this way. Perhaps the farm at Puddlehill grew into the solid stone-footed farm quarried away on the southern slopes of the hill.

There is no direct evidence of the early days of the town on the crossroads. We assume it had its origin in accommodation for travellers. By the second century it had expanded and was thriving; wells were dug on the outskirts of the built-up area, perhaps to serve industrial workshops as well as dwellings, but by the late fourth century all the wells so far located by archaeologists had gone out of use and been filled in. This suggests that the town had shrunk and no longer had need of them: they were plugged so that roaming children or animals could not fall into them. As time passed the fill

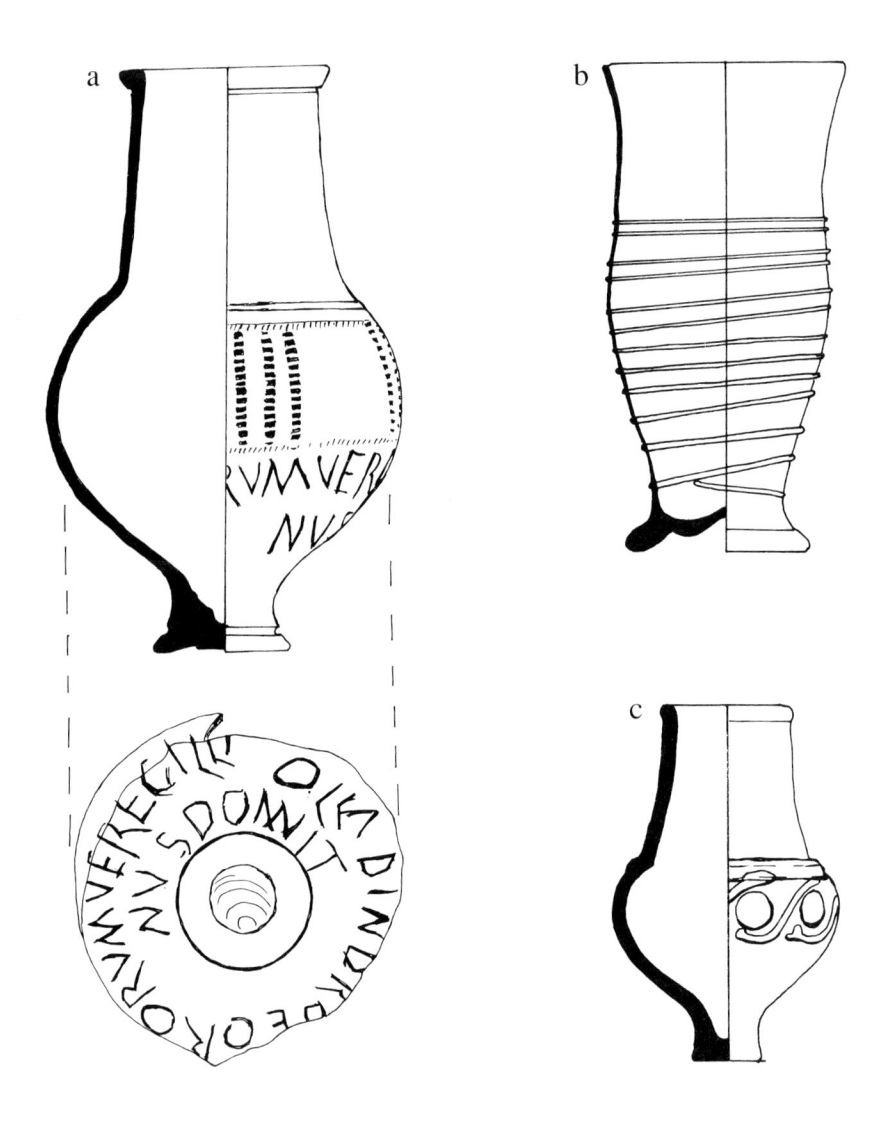

Fig. 37. Pottery and Glass found with Burials (Scale 1:2).
a   Inscribed pot
b   A delicate glass vessel
c   A little black cup, decorated in white, from a child's grave

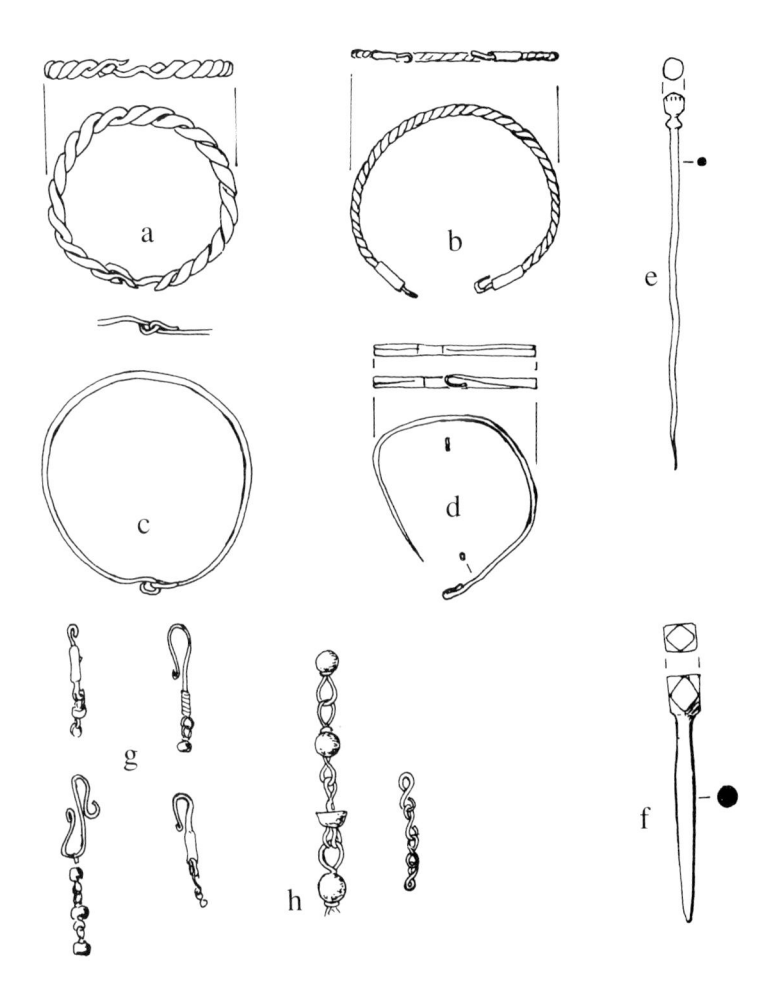

Fig. 38. Jewellery found in a little girl's grave (Scale 1:2, except *h* which is actual size).

a–d Four bracelets (there were seven in all). *a* and *b* are of twisted bronze and *b* was gilded.
e A bronze pin
f A jet pin
g, h Details of a necklace of coloured glass beads linked by bronze wire.

settled and subsided, so that the ground surface above sank into a hollow. At this point they were often used for burials, showing that people were still living (and dying) nearby, but that this area was considered as lying outside the town.

In the third century A.D. the Roman world underwent a catastrophic change. In the years 258–260 A.D. every frontier broke down; the Persians overran the eastern provinces, the Goths burst through the Dardanelles and across the Danube, wasted the Balkans and sacked Athens; the Moorish tribes raided Roman Africa and southern Spain, while, most devastating of all, the Franks and the Allemanni burst across the Rhine and ravaged all Roman Gaul, the first – and perhaps the most destructive – of all the great invasions of the Germans across the Rhine.

Although the invaders were driven back, the cost was enormous and the institutions of the early Empire perished. In the new Empire of the fourth century, the Emperors were generals commanding armies; it was no longer possible for one Government to rule the Empire from Rome. From separate capitals, Antioch or Constantinople in the east, Milan or Trier in the west, several Emperors ruled separate portions of the Empire as colleagues. The old frontier armies were reinforced with large, expensive mobile reserves billeted in towns. Twice the number of governments and twice the number of troops cost more money, and taxation weighed heavily on the later Empire.

Plate 14. Skeletons in top of well.

In the provinces there was no longer the distinction between Roman and Romanised natives on one hand, and non-Roman natives on the other. In 212 A.D. all free born inhabitants of the Empire had been made citizens of Rome; in the fourth century the legal grant became a social reality. The cobbler and ploughboy of Dunstable, of Yorkshire, or of Cornwall, were as fully Roman as their descendants are today English – though, of course, they felt no such strong national patriotism as the nationals of a single country feel today, for there were no comparable states like Rome beyond the frontiers.

In the great disaster of the third century, only Italy and Britain escaped invasion. From the disaster Britain emerged richer and more prosperous than before, and comparatively wealthier than northern Gaul and the Rhineland.

The fourth century was in general a prosperous period in Britain, with many fine villas built or refurbished, including the one at Totternhoe. Nevertheless there were threats from outside in the shape of raids on the coast and the northern frontier from the Picts in Scotland, the Scots in Ireland and the Saxons and other German tribes from across the North Sea. In 367 A.D. these forces combined, and spread chaos across Roman Britain. Slaves took their chance to escape and join in the pillage, and it was not till the following year when the general Theodosius was sent out that order was at last restored.

Perhaps Durocobrivis, an undefended town on a main road, suffered particularly badly at this time, and never fully recovered its former prosperity. This may account for its reduction in size in the late fourth century.

Verulamium survived as a city into the middle of the fifth century, long after Rome had left Britain to look after its own defences. These were dangerous times with government fragmented and barbarian raiders again taking their opportunity to overrun the countryside. It is doubtful if Durocobrivis could long survive in such conditions, but exactly how and when the town came to an end we do not know. We do know that the Roman town disappeared completely, and there is no evidence at all of early Saxon occupation of the site. Dunstable was not mentioned in Domesday Book and only re-emerged as a town under the patronage of Henry I in the early twelfth century.

Other Local Sites

Away from the towns – which were something quite new to the Britons – rural settlement seemed to continue much as before, but the population of Britain is believed to have risen to a level (a recent estimate is over 5 million) which it did not reach again until the sixteenth century. The evidence for this is the frequency with which scatters of Roman pottery, as well as actual stone foundations, turn up in ploughed fields and other sites all over the country. In our own town area evidence has been found in

Southfields, Graham Road, the Beecroft Estate and elsewhere, as well as in villages round about such as Totternhoe, Kensworth, Caddington and Tilsworth.

In Chalton, near Toddington, a valley site produces quantities of Romano-British material and ditches are visible there on air photos, but we have as yet found no building foundations.

Worthington Smith recorded interesting evidence from the Roman period in and around Maiden Bower. Outside the rampart of the Iron Age fort on the north-west side a number of Roman pots were found, at least four of them containing cremations. This must have been a second century cemetery. Inside the south entrance to Maiden Bower was a pit full of human bones – at least fifty individuals – jumbled together, and apparently dating from Roman times. Roman coins, pottery and jewellery (an intaglio) have also been found in the area, but no evidence of buildings.

Locations where Romano-British pottery or coins have been found in South Bedfordshire are too numerous to list here.

The Roman Villa at Totternhoe

Some of the great villas in south west Britain, built during the prosperity of the fourth century, were huge country mansions with fifty or seventy rooms on the ground floors. They were on a scale that can only compare with the building of the great mansions in England during the sixteenth and eighteenth centuries.

A large country house, unusually large for this area, was built during this prosperous period of Roman Britain at Totternhoe. The foundations still lie close beneath the surface of the field immediately south of Totternhoe Church.

A villa was not simply a luxury country residence: like the great houses of England in later centuries it was the centre of an estate, an economic unit deriving its income from the land around it.

Too little of the villa at Totternhoe has so far been excavated to reveal the overall plan of the buildings, domestic or agricultural, or the lay-out of the courtyard, still less the extent of the estate belonging to it. It is interesting to note, however, that the village church was later built close by, and a network of roads and paths seems to converge on this point. Is this coincidence, or did the villa lands later become an Anglo-Saxon estate, and later still a parish, still centred on the site where the owner's villa once stood?

The house is a type known as a "courtyard villa" (see plan Fig. 39); buildings were set around a central courtyard that had overall measurements of about 60 m × 70 m.

The southern boundary of this courtyard had been enclosed by a 120 cm thick flint wall and was entered through a gateway made of red sandstone. Added contrast in colour was provided by paving the gateway with white

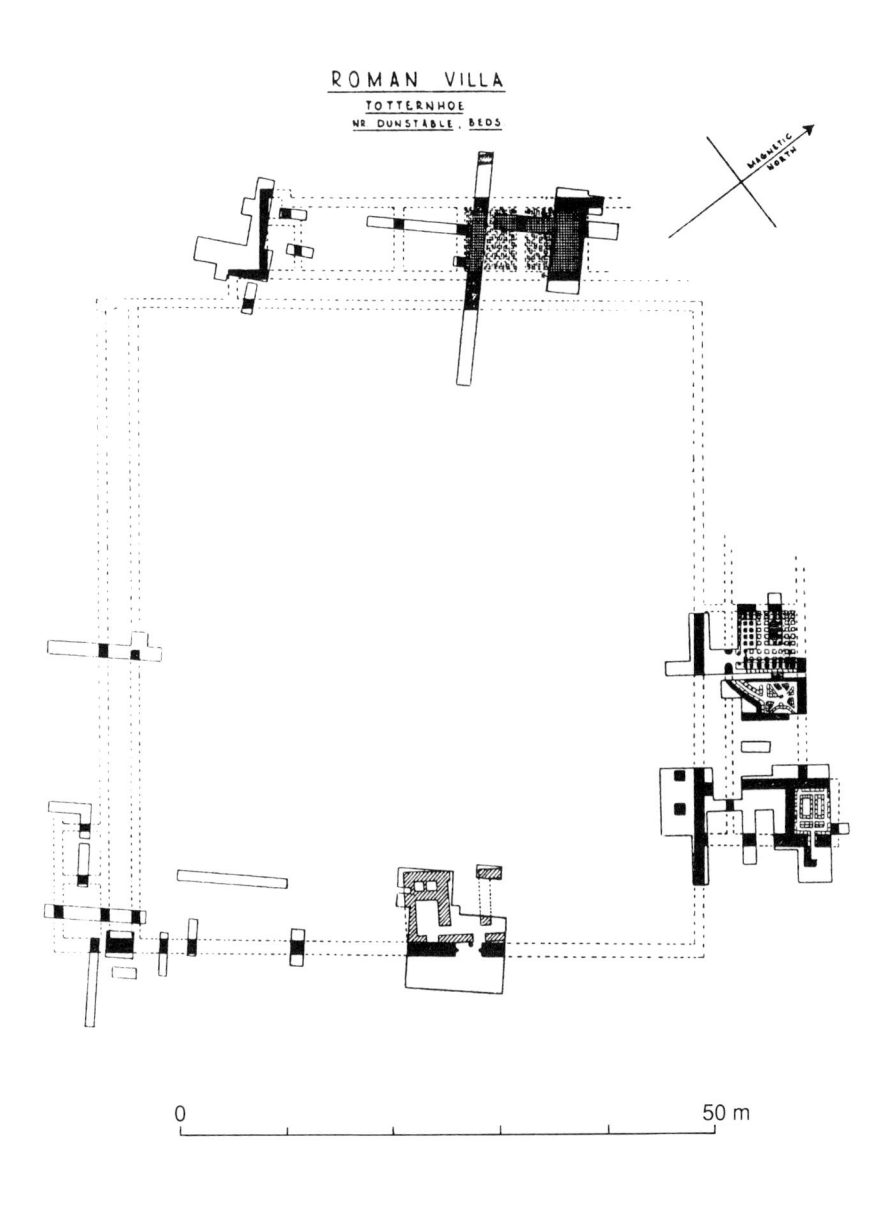

Fig. 39. Plan of Roman Villa at Totternhoe. Only parts of the building were excavated and these are shown on the plan. Dotted lines indicate the presumed position of walls in areas which were not excavated.

Plate 15. Totternhoe Roman villa hypocaust.

stone chippings, probably transported for the purpose from the other side of Bedford. Many of the rooms were centrally heated by hypocausts; hot air was circulated beneath floors laid on columns of tiles, this air being channelled up the walls by flues to escape into the atmosphere through the eaves of the buildings. The walls had flint bases up to a metre thick, and on the inside they were plastered and painted in gaudy colours.

Around the courtyard, linking the various rooms, was a 2.5 m wide verandah. This was roofed over and paved with a white tessellated floor. At the end of the eastern wing, entered through a columned doorway, was the bath block. This was built on the Turkish bath principle, with a very hot room, cool and cold rooms. This type of bathing was very much favoured by the Romans, and indeed was probably their favourite relaxation. Upper class Britons strove to adopt the manners and customs, as well as the technological advances, of Rome.

This was the house of a wealthy family: the owner may have been one of the local British aristocracy, a state official, or a rich merchant with a prosperous business in Durocobrivis or Verulamium.

Many bones and antlers of red deer suggest that the owner was fond of hunting, and also no doubt many an expedition was made from this building to visit the theatre at Verulamium. Gaming counters, beads and hairpins were among the many objects found within the building.

The pottery was predominantly of the fourth century, but it also contained an admixture of earlier sherds. A fine complete Samian dish was found. This belongs to the Antonine period (150–200 A.D.) and was made at Lezoux in Central Gaul by a potter using the stamp LIBERI. Another Samian dish of the same date was stamped POTTACI. On the side of this dish a Roman at Totternhoe had scratched the letters CVR, perhaps the owner's initials. The only other name we have from the building is "DOBALLUS". This potter's name was stamped four times on the rim of a large mortarium dish.

The presence of second century pottery suggests that there was a house on the site at that date, but the parts excavated were all later.

We do not know how many rooms the building contained, but they were probably divided into summer and winter apartments. During the winter, the owners must have lived in the rooms heated by hypocausts, and made cheerful with coloured and patterned mosaics.

In the summer, the unheated north block was used; this overlooked the courtyard with its flowerbeds, and had a view of the Chilterns as a background. The rooms were made to appear cooler by being paved with white tesserae bordered with a neat 12 cm wide band of soft grey. At the back of the rooms the grey stone tesserae had a ragged edge, in some places 45 cm wide. Obviously the floor on this side of the room had been covered by some kind of furnishing. Perhaps wooden cupboards stood here, or they

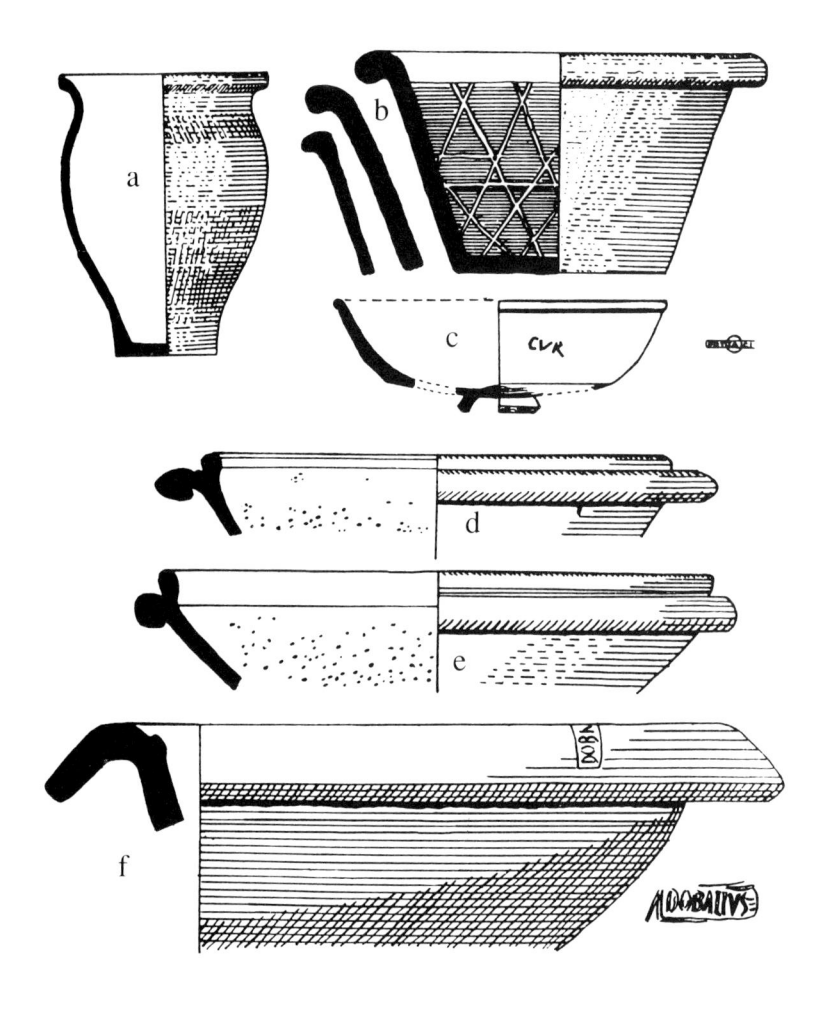

Fig. 40. Pottery from the Totternhoe Villa (Scale 1:4).
a, b   Cooking pots
c   Samian dish with stamp POTTACI
d, e   Examples of mortaria
f   Mortarium with a hooked rim, stamped DOBALLUS

86

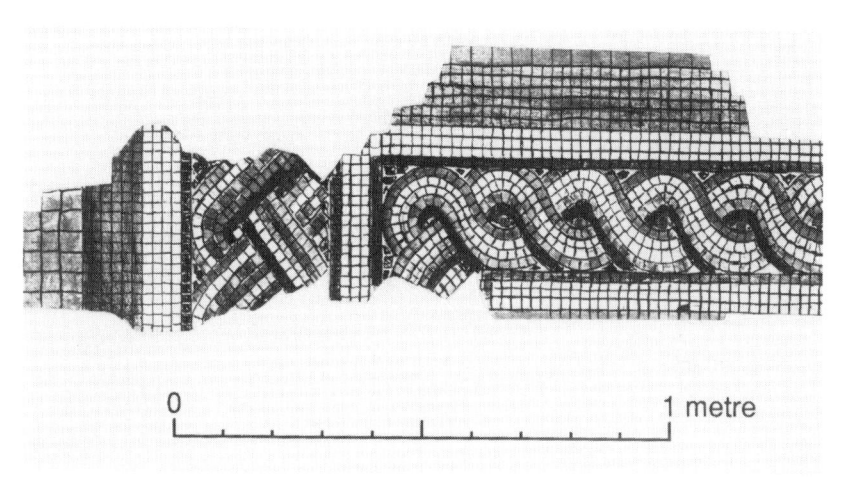

Plate 16. Part of a Mosaic Floor, Totternhoe Villa.

may have been bedrooms with a fixed couch on this side of the room, secured against the wall.

To travellers passing along the Icknield Way the house must have looked very cheerful standing on rising ground across the shallow valley with its roofs of red and yellow tiles, the black and white flint walls, and red sandstone gateway.

The fortunes of this great house changed over the years; additions were made during its history and then a gradual decay took place. Loose tesserae were swept out of the floors and repairs made with patches of cement. The west wing was burnt down and not rebuilt. This probably marked the end of the house as a country mansion. Internal walls were destroyed to make large barns. The tessellated pavements were covered with a rough, uneven layer of broken roof tile and flint, cemented to form very dry flooring. Such a floor would be admirably suitable for the storage of grain in sacks, allowing air to circulate beneath them.

This conversion of living rooms to barns is paralleled elsewhere in the late fourth century. Some villas even had corn-drying ovens dug through tessellated pavements. It may have been a sign of troubled times in the countryside, with the landowners departing to the safety of a town house and leaving a bailiff or tenant in charge of farming activities. Or the owners themselves may no longer have been wealthy: taxation was very heavy in the fourth century, when the Imperial Government had to maintain armies on many fronts. As the economy of Britain itself became increasingly disrupted by raiders from beyond its borders it may have become necessary for each villa estate to become self-sufficient, so that the production and storage of crops was all-important.

Plate 17. Tessellated floor covered by cobbling, Totternhoe Villa.

At Totternhoe the fronting wall of the courtyard was pulled down and the flint and sandstone of the gateway were used to construct a small double-winged cottage, slightly out of alignment with the wall.

A precise date for the end of the Totternhoe house cannot be given. Within its ruins we found sherds of hand-made pottery that belong to the Saxons of the fifth or sixth centuries. The fifth century in Britain heralds what are sometimes called the Dark Ages and the arrival of the first English. We shall return to the events of that period in the final chapter of this book.

A Building at Bidwell

No other villa has yet been found near Dunstable, but there are strong indications that one may lie to the north of Houghton Regis. Ploughing turned up a scatter of stone and tiles in a field there and a small excavation was carried out to investigate the site.

We found stone and flint walls from a small building. There was pottery of late Roman style, but not a great deal of it, or of other debris to suggest people had lived there.

Among the building materials were hollow curved box tiles (called "voussoirs") which had once formed part of a hot-air heating system and must have come from a substantial and elaborate building. These, the roofing tiles, painted wall plaster and other building materials must have been brought from elsewhere, probably a nearby villa, for use in this little building at Bidwell.

The site is a puzzling one. The chief mystery is the choice of situation. It is in the lowest part of the field, adjacent to a spring with permanent water less than a metre below the surface. The area is so wet that the flint walls had to be supported on a forest of wooden piles driven into the clay subsoil. The lower parts of these had survived well for 1,500 years, because they were permanently waterlogged: only the upper ends had partly rotted away. The sharpened points below were perfectly preserved, still showing the marks of the tool used to shape them.

Why construct a building on such a wet, difficult spot, when drier, rising ground was available all around? Perhaps the spring itself was the reason. The Celts often regarded springs and wells as sacred, each with a presiding deity and sometimes a shrine. The tradition persisted into Christian times in the form of "holy wells" with a reputation for healing and dedicated to a saint. "Well" as the second element of early English place names normally refers to a natural spring. Perhaps the one near this Roman site was important enough to give its name to the nearby hamlet of Bidwell.

Plate 18. Bidwell: Wooden piles preserved below the walls of a Roman building.

In the floor of the Roman structure a curious drain constructed of tiles and leading nowhere could perhaps have been for the reception of libations to the gods, or of water at a baptism.

    On some of the roof tiles a symbol had been drawn in the wet clay by the finger of whoever made them. This symbol could be interpreted as the Christian "chi rho" sign (the Greek initials of the name of Christ). Since we do not believe that the tiles were made specifically for the building, but came from a nearby villa, the link between this structure and Christian worship is very tenuous.

    The building was destroyed by fire, but as with Roman Dunstable and the Totternhoe villa we can put no date to its end.

Chapter 8

The Anglo-Saxon Settlements

The Decline of the Roman Empire

The coming of the pagan Saxons, the first Englishmen, is one of the most difficult of all historical problems. In the written records of Roman civilization the affairs of Britain are hardly noticed, and after 410 A.D. there are only one or two casual references during a century of voluminous records.

It is still a widely held belief that in the year 410 A.D. the Roman Legions marched down the Watling Street and left Britain. It is true that there can have been little in the way of a Roman army in Britain after 410, but the undermining of the military strength of Britain probably started in the year 367, when the armies of Britain were destroyed by the joint attack of Picts from the highlands of Scotland, Scots from Ireland and Saxons from Germany.

Ten years later the armies of the east in the Roman Empire were destroyed by a Teutonic confederation of tribes headed by the Goths. The position was restored by the Emperor Theodosius (the son of the General who had campaigned in Britain in 368 A.D.). He had to adopt the expedient of accepting the services of bands of barbarians, mainly Goths, who operated under their own chiefs, bound only by an oath of loyalty to the Emperor. These armies were settled within the frontiers of the Roman State. It was this practice of employing barbarian troops under their own chieftains that eventually led to the conquest of Britain by the barbarian Saxons.

Theodosius died in 395 A.D. His two sons were already enthroned as joint Emperors, Arcadius in Constantinople, and Honorius, under the guardianship of Theodosius' general Stilicho, a German, in Rome. In the late 390s Stilicho organised the defences of Britain. When this was completed some of his troops returned to the continent. After a very confused and violent series of events the eastern Empire (controlled from Constantinople) expelled the Goths from its provinces.

The western Empire could do no such thing, and a Gothic host marched and counter-marched throughout the Balkans and Italy. It was led by Alaric who was a Gothic king by birth, and who was at the same time a Roman commander-in-chief by virtue of a commission extracted from the Imperial Government. Honorius completely lost control of the situation and withdrew his court from Rome to Ravenna, a town tucked away in the marshes. The end of the western Roman Empire came very rapidly after this. Following various lesser German raids, a host of Vandals, Alans and Sueves crossed the Rhine at the end of December in the year 406. Unlike other invaders they were never driven back and they effectively cut communications between

Britain and Italy. Thereafter Britain proclaimed her own Emperors, two of whom were murdered within a few months. The third, Constantine III, took his troops over to Gaul, where he drove the bulk of the invaders southwards towards Spain. His principal general, Gerontius, is explicitly described as a Briton, and Constantine may well have been British himself. Their names survive as Geraint and Kysteint among those commonly used by Dark Age British kinglets.

A new Imperial Government fought and defeated Constantine and conducted long-drawn-out, two-faced negotiations with Alaric. Alaric lost his patience and in the year 410 seized and plundered the city of Rome. Thereupon a complex pattern of plot, counterplot and rebellion ensued. In the course of this Honorius sent written orders to the cities of Britain instructing them to see to their own defence. The phrase is unusual and informal and marks the permanent end of the political control of Britain by the Roman Imperial Government.

The Coming of the Saxons

The inability of Honorius to send troops to defend his outlying provinces marked the end not only of Roman Britain but of the Roman Empire in the west. It did not, however, mean the end of Roman civilization in Britain. Phrases like "the withdrawal of the legions" and "the end of the Roman occupation" have encouraged the idea that in or about 410 A.D. the Romans made a mass exodus from Britain, leaving the defenceless natives behind. It may be stated most emphatically that there is no evidence of any such evacuation, if only because there was no longer any real distinction between "Romans" and "natives". There was, of course, a wide social gap between a peasant and a landowner, but all natives (except slaves) were Romans, and all but a fraction of the Romans were natives. This fraction consisted of two elements: a handful of senior civilian officials (those of whom we know were for the most part Syrians, Gauls or German Romans) and a proportion of the army whose size it is not possible to estimate, but who were of barbarian German birth, some of whom may have been settled as half-free farmers liable to military service. There appear to have been very few "Romans" here who actually came from Rome or Italy.

The virtual silence of continental writers about affairs in Britain after the year 410 A.D. is the most eloquent witness that in this year the province was decisively and permanently severed from the Roman political state. Our knowledge from this year depends on marrying up the British written records with the archaeological evidence.

Even if we had no written evidence at all for the events of the fourth and fifth centuries, we should know from the record left in the soil that some catastrophe had overcome the people of this country, their towns and their villas, and that new inhabitants with a totally different way of life had moved in. The Roman invasion in the first century brought changes that must have amazed the native Britons, who had never seen metalled roads, building bricks, central heating, bathrooms, writing, bureaucracy and all the other innovations brought by a great civilized empire. Four hundred years later nearly all these changes were reversed – in some places with sudden violence, elsewhere by slow decay.

The Literary Evidence

Few written records which describe the coming of the Saxons have survived. The newcomers were illiterate and no contemporary Saxon accounts of the early settlements exist.

The best known written source for the "Dark Ages" of Britain is Bede's "Ecclesiastical History of the English People" completed in 730 A.D. Bede was an English monk, writing in Northumbria. His history proper opens in 597 when Saint Augustine landed at Thanet, commissioned by Pope Gregory the Great to convert "the heathen English". In his introductory chapters, however, he sketches the previous history of Britain, and he deals with the Roman period and with certain events in the fifth century in considerable detail. Unfortunately he makes an abrupt jump from 450 when he says the first Saxons landed (though we know this date should in fact be earlier), to the arrival of Saint Augustine one hundred and fifty years later. He does, however, state that the immigrants consisted of Saxons, Angles and Jutes and that the Saxons came from Old Saxony (the land between the Rhine and the Elbe), the Angles from Angeln (East Schleswig) and the Jutes from Jutland (probably by way of Frisia).

One of the main sources for Bede's narrative of this period was a tract written by a British monk called Gildas. Gildas was writing around 540 A.D. and his main concern was to denounce the evils of his day, but this is the one near-contemporary work that has survived. It is he who tells us that the Saxons were invited into Britain to repel the invading Picts and Scots, and that after they had completed this task they "were settled in the eastern part of Britain". Writing as a native Briton, clinging to the remnants of the heritage of Rome, which had brought civilization and Christianity to the country, he looked upon these unwanted heathen immigrants – "the vile unspeakable Saxons" he calls them "hated of God and man alike" – as a terrible punishment on the sins of the Britons.

It was not until the reign of Alfred the Great that the oral traditions of the English were set down in writing. The Anglo-Saxon Chronicle, which was compiled in the latter half of the ninth century (a hundred and fifty years later than Bede), was an attempt to preserve and reconcile the legends that had been handed down over a span of nearly four hundred years. Its treatment of the happenings of the fifth and sixth centuries, with which we are concerned, is not a detailed account of contemporary history but a catalogue of isolated and dimly remembered events, assigned by guesswork to particular dates.

Although divided into different tribes, and later separate kingdoms, the immigrants acknowledged a relationship to each other and to their German kinsfolk left behind on the continent, and they spoke dialects of a Germanic language. We often call them collectively "Anglo-Saxons", keeping the term "English" for their descendants of later centuries. The native Britons called them all "Saxons" (in Scottish "Sassenach" and in Welsh "Saesen"). They came to call themselves and their language "English" after their homeland in Angeln, and called their new country "England".

The people they found here had been known as Britons (or variants of this term) since prehistoric times, but in the fifth century they began to call themselves "Combrogi" which meant "fellow-countrymen" to distinguish themselves from the foreign newcomers. This has developed into modern Welsh "Cymry", with "Cymru" as the name of their land. The English arrogantly referred to them as "Welsh", a Germanic word for "foreigner", which in England also took on the meaning "slave", but in parts of the country where relations between the peoples were better they used the native word, and it appears in place-names such as Cumberland and Comberton. These native Britons spoke the Celtic British language which has developed into modern Welsh. Latin was evidently not widely enough spoken in Roman Britain to survive into post-Roman times, except as the language of the Church and of written records.

The Original Settlements

The main outlines of the story of the Saxon invasion are related by Gildas and Bede. Britain was being raided by the Picts from beyond the Forth and the Clyde, the Scots from Ireland, and Saxon pirates along the east coast. According to Gildas, Vortigern, a British king, adopted the Roman expedient of hiring Saxon mercenaries to protect Britain from these raiders. Early Germanic sites attributable to such mercenaries have been found in southeast Yorkshire, Lincolnshire, East Anglia and Kent – strategic points for defence against raiders from the sea. As we shall see, Luton may also have been one of these military settlements.

The Saxons did their job. They drove out the Picts and the Scots and settled in Britain, but they greatly reinforced their original numbers by boatloads of new immigrants until they were strong enough to dictate their own terms to the Britons. A dispute arose – Gildas says that it was about their rations – and they mutinied against their employers. Bands of Saxons devastated the countryside, looted the towns and harried the Britons from coast to coast. Bede describes the plight of the latter: "A few wretched survivors captured in the hills were butchered wholesale... Some fled overseas in their misery; others clinging to their homeland, eked out a wretched and fearful existence among the mountains, forests and crags, ever on the alert for danger." There is no doubt that the Saxon revolt wrecked what survived by the mid 5th century of the material basis of Roman civilization in Britain.

There is just one contemporary reference to these events by a continental writer: a Gaulish chronicler states that in about 442 A.D. "Britain passed into the control of the Saxons".

The Britons, however, successfully rallied under Ambrosius Aurelianus, and after a long series of campaigns of varying fortunes, defeated the English armies. A decisive victory was won by the British at the battle of Mount Badon, probably fought somewhere in Wessex – there are several candidates for the actual site – about the year 500. For fifty years the British in the affected region were not further troubled and to Gildas, the Saxon threat was a thing of the past, though he speaks of a land partitioned between the two peoples.

The Archaeological Evidence

The few written sources can only be filled out by inferences from archaeology. This at least is tangible evidence, but even so it presents special difficulties. The Romans generally built in stone, hoarded and mislaid coins, used mass-produced pottery and raised inscribed tombstones over their dead. These features of their civilization have survived on the sites where the Romans actually lived and they can be closely dated.

After 400 A.D., although the Romano-British population of this densely inhabited land did not disappear, the datable evidence for them did. New coins ceased to reach Britain and in the troubled times of raids, fragmented government and economic chaos, the mass-production of pottery came to an end. Thus it is no longer possible to date archaeological sites by coins and pottery. Both probably continued in use and re-use for years, but we cannot say how long.

In Verulamium, Professor Frere excavated a building which, subsequent to the year 380 (dated by a coin found beneath a floor), underwent a number of alterations and changes of use, culminating in the laying of a water-main. All this takes us up to the mid fifth century, when the city water supply must still have been in working order. There is also written evidence for a visit to the shrine of Saint Alban 429 A.D. by Bishop Germanus from the Continent, when he found Verulamium still a city with wealthy inhabitants.

Elsewhere we search in vain for evidence of the Romano-British population in the years following the end of Roman rule. Once the mass of the people became Christian, burials ceased to be accompanied by grave offerings, depriving the archaeologist of another source of information. It is only in the last few years that very careful excavation of the latest layers of

Roman sites has begun to produce evidence from these "post-Roman" or "sub-Roman" years.

The early Saxons, on the other hand, had very distinctive forms of burial, and for many years their cemeteries provided nearly the whole of our evidence for their culture. In the early cemeteries three clearly marked methods of burial are evident. From Norfolk to Yorkshire the Anglian peoples who first settled there always cremated their dead and buried their ashes in urns. This had been the custom of their Teutonic forefathers and they continued to observe it in their new homeland. All uncremated burials are later in date. In Kent by the sixth century straightforward burial (technically termed inhumation) was the rule. This was the Roman practice and it had been adopted by all German peoples in Roman service and more generally in contact with Rome. Finally, over a wide area, which included the Icknield Way sites and a number of cemeteries in Surrey, both cremation and inhumation burials took place simultaneously.

Fortunately the pagan Anglo-Saxons buried a rich variety of grave goods with their dead, and some of the urns, brooches and other objects can be approximately dated. Early developments of certain types of brooch are common to both England and the German homelands, and belong to the fifth century (e.g. Fig. 41 *a*). Later developed types are found in England but not in Germany. The ultimate developments of these brooches are found in graves which can be dated by late sixth and early seventh century coins.

The earliest types of Anglo-Saxon brooches ever found in Britain come from a cemetery at Kempston, outside Bedford, and from one at Argyll

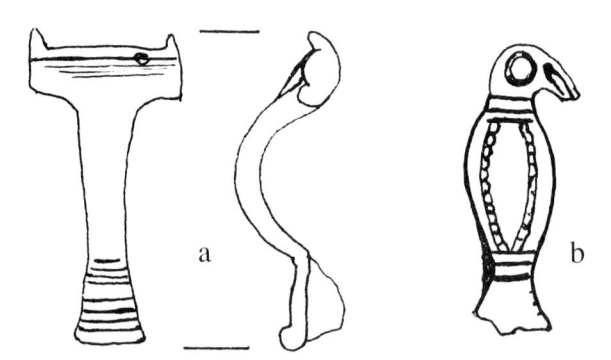

Fig. 41. Early Saxon Bronze Brooches from Argyll Avenue Cemetery in Luton (Actual size). *a*, Brooch of a type also found in Germany and dated around 400 A.D. One of the earliest Anglo-Saxon objects found in Britain. *b*, Bird brooch of the later fifth century.

Fig. 42. Cremation Urn from Argyll Avenue Cemetery (Scale 1:4). This type, decorated with bosses, is also found in Germany and is called a "Buckelurne" from the German word for "boss" or "hump". It dates from the early fifth century.

Avenue, in Luton. It may be that these are the cemeteries of Saxons invited in by the Britons in the early fifth century, billeted in Bedfordshire to cover the important crossing of the Watling Street and the Icknield Way and to serve as a striking force in support of other troops along the east coast and the Thames Valley.

Apart from these two cemeteries, another at Sandy and a possible one at Toddington, there is little evidence of a Saxon presence in the whole Chiltern region, or the flatter lands to the north, until the end of the sixth century. It seems that the British remained in control here and English settlement was not permitted.

The Britons Retaliate: The Saxon Warrior on Puddlehill

Very little is known of what happened during the confused fighting in the years before the British victory at Mount Badon c.500 A.D., but at some point there were probably clashes in our locality. On the highest point of Puddlehill an early Saxon warrior lay buried (Plate 19 and cover). He had been killed by a savage blow above his left ear which had smashed his skull. He was so tall that he had to be squeezed into his grave which was itself fully six feet long – his heels were jammed against one end, his head forced forward at the other and his spine was slightly twisted. He had been buried by his compatriots in the true pagan tradition, with his shield and his spear. The shield was made from wood, probably covered with hide. In the centre was a pointed iron boss, held to the shield with iron rivets and bronze washers. Traces of the wood still survived beneath these rivets. There was a shield grip, an iron bar beneath the centre boss. Four separate rivets had been used to secure leather straps on the inside of the shield and with them was a small iron buckle. These had been used to strap the shield to his forearm during battle, or to secure it over his shoulder when not in use. At his waist was an iron ring, and a short distance away a small knife. The knife had been carried in a sheath hung from his belt by the iron ring. It was a domestic knife of a type commonly carried by the pagan Saxons.

Lying near his head was the iron socket of his spear. The point of this weapon was missing and it had probably been broken off in battle. Small wood fibres, the remains of the spear shaft, still survived in the socket.

The grave was very shallow and had been dug across an earlier Romano-British ditch. From the position of the shield boss, the edge of the shield must have been lying on the natural chalk which here is covered by only 15 cm of soil. The burial must therefore have been covered by an earth mound. Under the same mound, in a grave barely deep enough for him to be covered, was the skeleton of another man, whose left leg had been severed just above the knee. Whether he was buried at the same time as the warrior we do not know. There were several more graves surrounding the mound but these had not been dug until a century or more later.

Plate 19. Saxon Warrior, Puddlehill.

We do not know what the victorious Britons did about the Saxons they had defeated. The grave goods of the early sixth century found in Kent, Sussex, Wessex, East Anglia and the North are plentiful enough to prove that Saxons continued to live and die in Britain. At Luton, for instance, burials if not cremations continued uninterrupted. On the other hand no Saxon remains of this period have been identified in the wide stretch of country between the deserted Chilterns and the Thames; eastwards from Luton along the Icknield Way there is no known burial for thirty miles until the immediate neighbourhood of Cambridge. This suggests that the Britons could not expel the Saxons, but they were contained in isolated groups either under British rule or bound to keep the peace by treaty or the threat of force. When the Saxons broke through again they had to liberate or re-occupy sites that they had settled previously. This certainly applies to the settlements along the Icknield Way.

During the next fifty years there is evidence of a hardening of the frontiers of areas of Anglo-Saxon settlement, with very little mixing or movement from one area to another.

The Saxon Conquest

The precarious peace was shattered in 552 when Ceawlin (Colin) a prince of the West Saxons on the Upper Thames, won a battle near Salisbury. His subsequent campaigns in the West Country made him master of Wessex which, by the end of his reign, comprised Berkshire, Hampshire, Wiltshire, Oxfordshire and a large part of Gloucestershire. He seems to have fought British and rival Saxons during his reign, before it ended in unspecified confusion and disaster in 593. In 571, however, the English under the leadership of Cutha (of the royal house of Wessex) won a decisive victory over the "Brit-Welsh" at "Bedcanford". Bedcanford has caused a lot of trouble. It sounds like Bedford, but Bedford at this time would have been spelt "Bedeanford" – the ford of Bieda who perhaps lived at Biddenham nearby. Bedford fits the archaeological evidence, but unless the discrepancy can be explained by the mis-spelling of a scribe as he copied an ill-written manuscript, place-name experts will not allow the identification.

Wherever the victory took place, it opened the Icknield Way to the Saxons. They broke through and captured Lygeanburg (Limbury, where we noted a Romano-British settlement in the previous chapter and near the Biscot Mill Saxon cemetery), Aegelesburg (Aylesbury), Baenesingtun (Benson, near Dorchester-on-Thames) and Egonesham (Eynsham, near Oxford). The British territory which separated the Saxons in Cambridgeshire and Bedfordshire from those west of the middle Thames was thus overrun and the whole belt of country from the southern edge of the East Anglian fens along the Chilterns to the Upper Thames was now in Saxon hands.

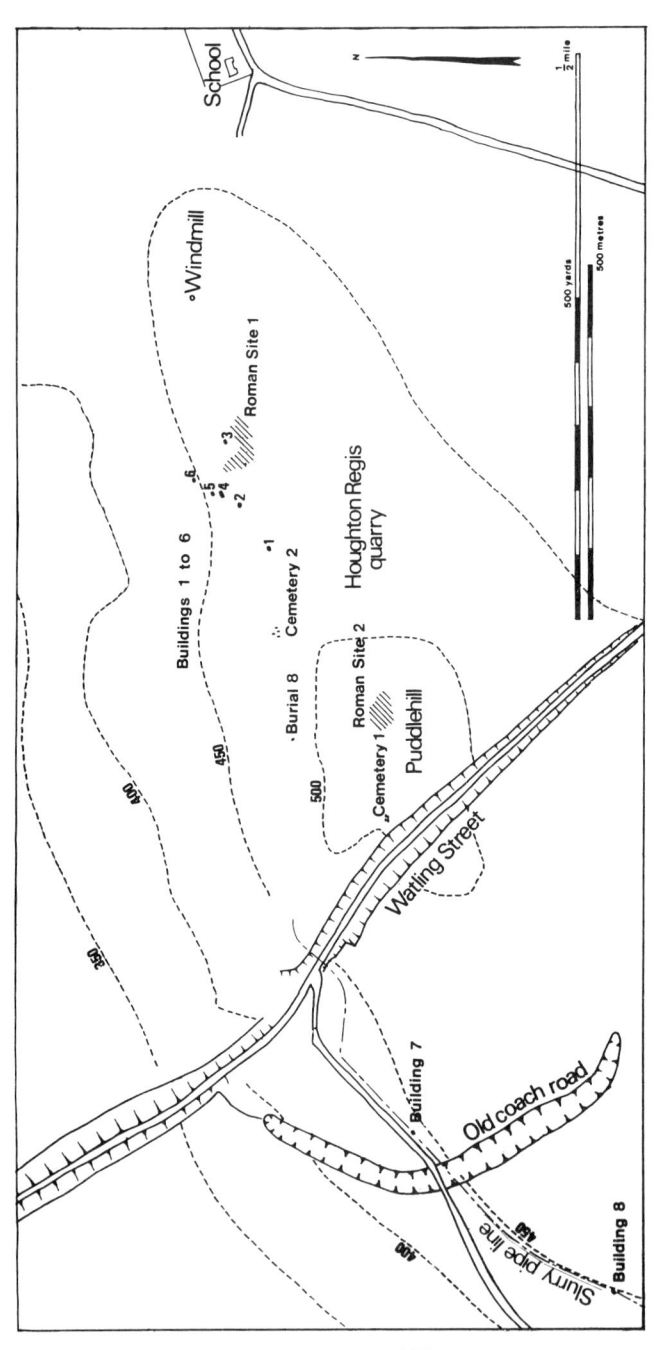

Fig. 43. Saxon Sites north of Dunstable.
The Saxon Warrior was buried in Cemetery 1.
The woman buried with her jewellery was buried in Cemetery 2.
(Contours in feet).

These events paved the way for the appearance of Saxon settlements and cemeteries all over our region from the late sixth century onwards.

By the year 600 the Saxons had established no less than ten separate – and sometimes hostile – kingdoms south of the Humber. With the exception of Wales, the Devon-Cornwall peninsula and certain isolated British kingdoms, the English conquest had been achieved.

Saxon Settlement on Puddlehill

Over the past twenty-five years archaeologists have learned a good deal more than they used to know about how and where the English settlers actually lived. Once again Puddlehill has contributed to that knowledge.

On most Anglo-Saxon settlement sites there are two types of structure: substantial wooden halls, interpreted as dwelling houses, and small rectangular buildings with floors excavated below ground level, believed to have been workshops or similar outbuildings. We have found none of the large halls locally, but two of the Puddlehill sunken-floored structures were large enough to have been family homes.

The earliest Saxon building so far excavated near Dunstable was found on the north slope of Puddlehill to the west of Watling Street, near the lane leading to Sewell. It dates to the late sixth century, part of the expansion of English settlement after the Wessex victories of this period.

It was found, along with one other of later date, when a 1.2 m wide pipe-trench was cut through the field, and there are probably others lying nearby awaiting discovery. Among the finds from its sunken floor was a small pot decorated with stamped rosettes (Fig. 44). After about 600 A.D. the domestic Saxon pottery was nearly always plain and undecorated, and this was the kind found in the other Puddlehill houses. These people had not learned the use of a potter's wheel, so there is some similarity between their products and the plain wares of the Early Iron Age. One difference is the use, increasing in the seventh century, of chopped grass or chaff to temper the clay. It has been suggested that in fact horse-dung was being mixed with

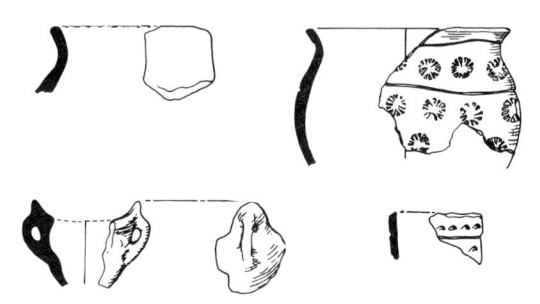

Fig. 44. Late Sixth Century Pots from Building 8 near Sewell Lane (Scale 1:4).

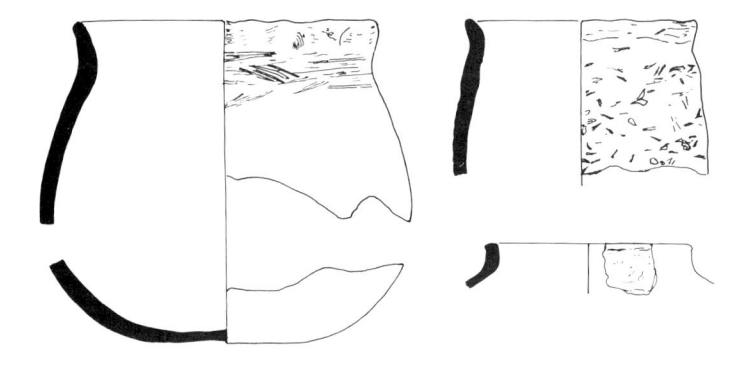

Fig. 45. Seventh Century pottery from farmstead on Puddlehill (Scale 1:4).

the clay, making it easier to mould and less likely to crack while being fired (they did not use kilns but bonfires). The majority of the pots are of a very low standard of manufacture (e.g. Fig. 45). A modern infants' class in pottery would produce better vessels within the first term. This was not for the lack of examples of better pots, as the ground was littered with pot sherds from the Romano-British occupation and sherds of these "good" wares were found within the Saxon buildings. The use of pottery may have played only a small part in the economy of the Saxon household, with lathe-turned wooden platters, bowls and cups being the main tableware, but the lack of craftsmanship in the making of these cooking and storage pots never ceases to surprise. It is quite usual, except in the earliest period, to find that the domestic pottery is aesthetically far inferior to the vessels used for funerary purposes. These were often lavishly decorated. However, these hand-made domestic wares were probably very serviceable for the purposes for which they were intended.

One other isolated Saxon sunken-floored structure has been identified to the west of Watling street. This was destroyed by the Sewell chalk quarry.

To the east of Watling Street the Saxon settlement was on the northern slope of Puddlehill, above Houghton Regis and quite near the site of a Roman farmstead. Two generations of people lived there during the seventh century, perhaps from about 625 onwards, and they buried their dead nearby.

The largest structure, called Building 4 (Fig. 46) was 9.15 m long and 4.25 m wide, its floor sunk 20 cm into the chalk ground. Five strong posts supported the ridge, perhaps because the roof was made of heavy turves, and there was a porched entrance at the north-west corner. This was probably the family home, but a smaller building, No. 5, seems to be contemporary with it. In size and structure this is more typical of the usual Saxon sunken-floored huts: roughly 4 m by 3.5 m, and with a large posthole at each

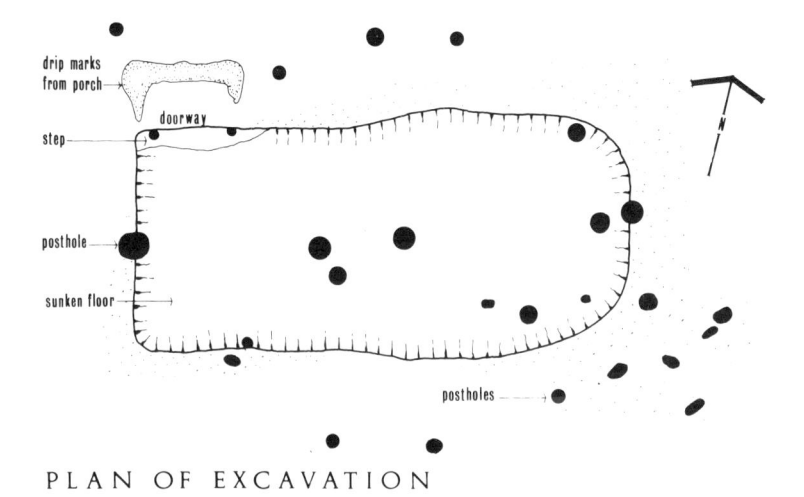

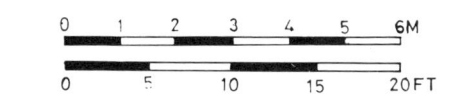

Fig. 46. Saxon Building 4, Puddlehill. Plan, and an artist's impression of how it may have been constructed.

Plate 20. Saxon Building 5, Puddlehill. The column of earth left standing in the floor is not part of the original structure. It was preserved by the archaeologists to show the layers filling the sunken area.

end (Plate 20). Less typically Building 5 had additional posts each side, sloping in towards the ridge, again perhaps to carry a heavy roof.

The chalk that was dug out when these houses were constructed must have been built up to make a surrounding wall, perhaps with timbers set into the top of it. The end posts carried a ridge-pole, and rafters resting on the walls would meet at the ridge. The roof could have been thatched, but, as we have noted, the size of some of the supports in these buildings suggests something heavier, probably turf.

Digging on the hill, summer and winter, for 17 years, showed the archaeologists how inhospitable this site could be for the greater part of the year and made them realise how practical and, during the winter, how comfortable these sunken-floored, turf-roofed buildings could have been. The people truly lived insulated by the ground, protected from the winds that consistently sweep across the site.

When these buildings were abandoned and the roofs fell in, the sites were marked by low mounds, suggesting the remains of heavy turf roofs lying on the collapsed walls. These mounds are still visible in the twentieth century, and at least one of them awaits excavation.

Building 3 was a bakehouse with a clay-lined oven dug out from one side. Saxon sunken-floored structures elsewhere in the country sometimes show evidence of a boarded floor at ground level, leaving a hollow space beneath. However, this does not seem to have been the case on Puddlehill. It would have been impossible in the bakehouse, where the oven was dug partly below ground level.

The chalk walls of some of these structures were rough-hewn, showing no signs of wear and may have been protected inside by wattle walling. Building 6 (Fig. 47) actually had a continuous row of stake holes running round inside the chalk wall and a double row at one end, which suggests woven hurdles lining the interior. It also raises the question: where was the doorway? Only Building 4 had a recognisable entrance. The others may have had a small way in high in a gable end, with wooden steps down to the floor.

No fireplaces were found either, but if most of the structures were workshops or sheds this is less surprising. Building 5 was remarkable for the number of stake holes of unknown purpose dotted all over the floor. It also had a groove in the floor along one side which may have accommodated the base and weights of an upright loom, or the feet of the weavers.

The dwelling house of the second generation of the settlement (Building 1) was of a more elaborate design, unknown elsewhere. Its sunken floor was 6 m long, but there were also postholes surrounding it and drip-marks from the roof which show that it was boat-shaped and nearly 12 m long in all. In

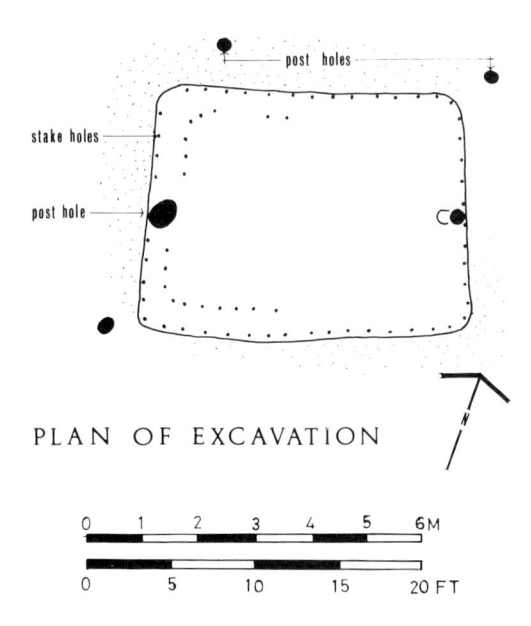

Fig. 47. Saxon Building 6, Puddlehill.

the report on the site (see Book List) Mrs. Sonia Hawkes says "The impression one gets from this house is of a snug and practical dwelling, well adapted to entertaining, individually designed by a man of ingenuity who knew his local weather all too well."

Mrs. Hawkes suggests that Building 6 (5.8 m by 4.5 m) might have served as a "bower" (Old English "bur"), a guest house or private quarters for the womenfolk. One of the finds was a broken cowrie shell of a species found in the Red Sea and eastwards. These were used as amulets or lucky charms, probably for fertility and childbirth, and are often found in the graves of women or children (as in the Marina Drive cemetery described below). Perhaps one use of this house was for women at times of childbirth. The floor was worn smooth by people's feet in the centre, but not round the edges, suggesting that benches or other furniture were fixed against the woven wattle walls.

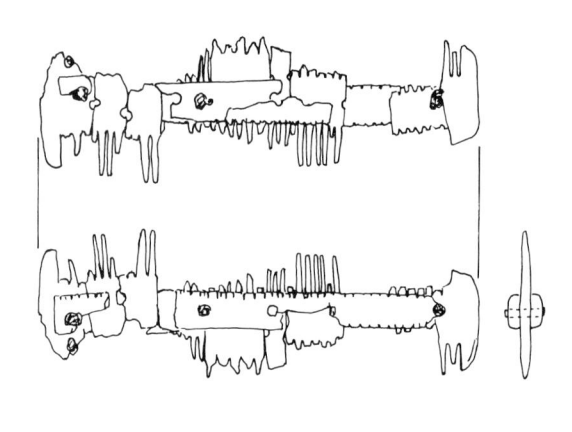

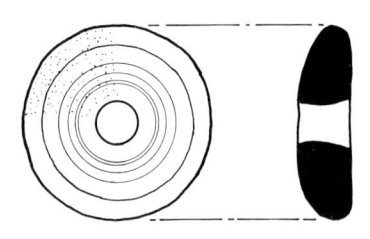

Fig. 48. Comb (unfinished – not all the teeth have been cut) and Spindle Whorl. Both made of bone (Scale 1:2).

Life on the Saxon Farmstead

In many ways these early English farmers in their simple wooden homes were living a similar life on Puddlehill to the Iron Age Celts a thousand years earlier, farming the land and making their own clothes and pots.

The evidence suggests that they relied on rearing animals rather than growing crops. Bones of cattle, sheep, pigs and fowls were found. They also kept horses and dogs. If they did not grow their own crops they must have traded their animal products for corn to make their bread. The sheep were not primarily kept for wool as most were slaughtered young; nevertheless finds of spindle whorls, finely made on a lathe, polished and decorated with grooves, show that the women were spinning wool on the site (Fig. 48). There were also bone tools used in weaving and other bone pins and needles.

It seems that everyone, man, woman and child, carried a personal iron knife, usually in a sheath at the waist, point upwards. Several were found on Puddlehill and they accompany very many Saxon burials, sometimes as the only item.

Decorated bone combs are frequent finds on Saxon sites (suggesting some care about personal appearance). An unfinished one found in Building 4 may mean that they were being manufactured there (Fig. 48).

Two finds from the settlement show us that the people living there could afford a little luxury: one is the imported cowrie shell and the other a circular disc, perhaps a box-lid, decorated with silver.

When we look at the jewellery belonging to one of the women buried in their graveyard we may even talk of wealth.

Puddlehill Saxon Cemetery

We have already considered the burial of the early sixth century warrior and the other graves surrounding him, but nearer to the Saxon houses was another little cemetery, where four widely-spaced burials were found. It seems probable that these were of people from the homestead.

One grave within this group proved to be a rich burial. A woman had been buried face downwards in a shallow grave in the full array of her wealth. Across her chest she wore a collar of eighty beads; forty-nine were amber and the rest were opaque glass, many decorated with different coloured inlays. The collar had been secured at each shoulder by two magnificent saucer brooches nearly 8 cm in diameter (Fig. 49 and Plate 21). They were cast in bronze and had traces of gilding. On the backs of these brooches were bronze catchplates and a mass of rust, presumably the corroded remains of iron pins. These saucer brooches are the ultimate development in England of the small brooches found in fifth century graves. The beads are of continental manufacture, perhaps coming from the Mediterranean region. In 1931 similar beads were found near Leighton Buzzard during sand digging at the Chamberlains Barn pit (Cemetery I), where there must have been

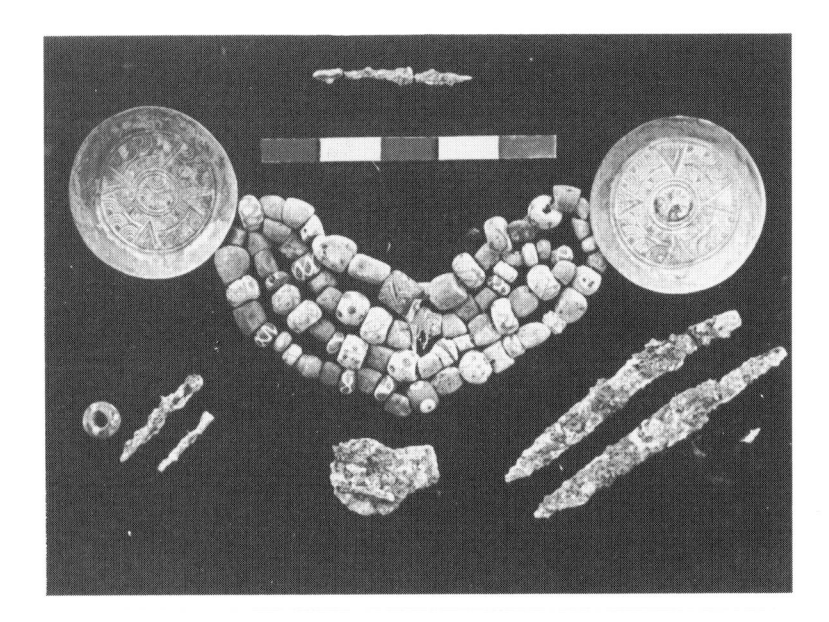

Plate 21. Jewellery, two knives and other items from the burial of a rich Anglo-Saxon Woman.

burials of the same sort of date as this one. The amber probably came from the Baltic. The Puddlehill brooches and beads had been backed with leather, some of which had survived, as it was impregnated with iron oxide from the pins.

At her waist lay a belt buckle and a knife that had probably once hung in a leather sheath from her belt. By her left hand she had a second knife and two small iron points, probably the remains of a little tool-kit in a pouch. The latter may have been decorated with a large red bead inlaid with white, yellow and blue, which lay alongside. Mrs. Hawkes describes this burial as an "outstandingly rich grave for its period."

The style of jewellery identifies the wearer as a West Saxon who died before the middle of the seventh century. She was buried wearing the "national costume" of a straight woollen tunic pinned at each shoulder with a brooch, a festoon of beads hanging between. The evidence of a leather backing suggests they may have been fastened to a bib or yoke of leather over her dress.

She and her family must have been people of some importance and may be part of a deliberate colonisation of these West Saxon frontier lands after the expansion of Wessex in the late sixth century. Bedfordshire remained a borderland between the Anglo-Saxon kingdoms of Wessex and Mercia for several centuries. Houghton Regis (in which Puddlehill lies) was a royal

Fig. 49. Saucer Brooch. One of the pair worn by a Saxon woman buried on Puddlehill (Actual size).

manor (hence "regis"), as were Luton and Leighton Buzzard also, forming a large block of royal lands across South Bedfordshire. It could be that royal ownership dates back to the original sixth century conquest of the area from the British by the Wessex royal family, and that our Puddlehill lady was one of a privileged colony deliberately settled there.

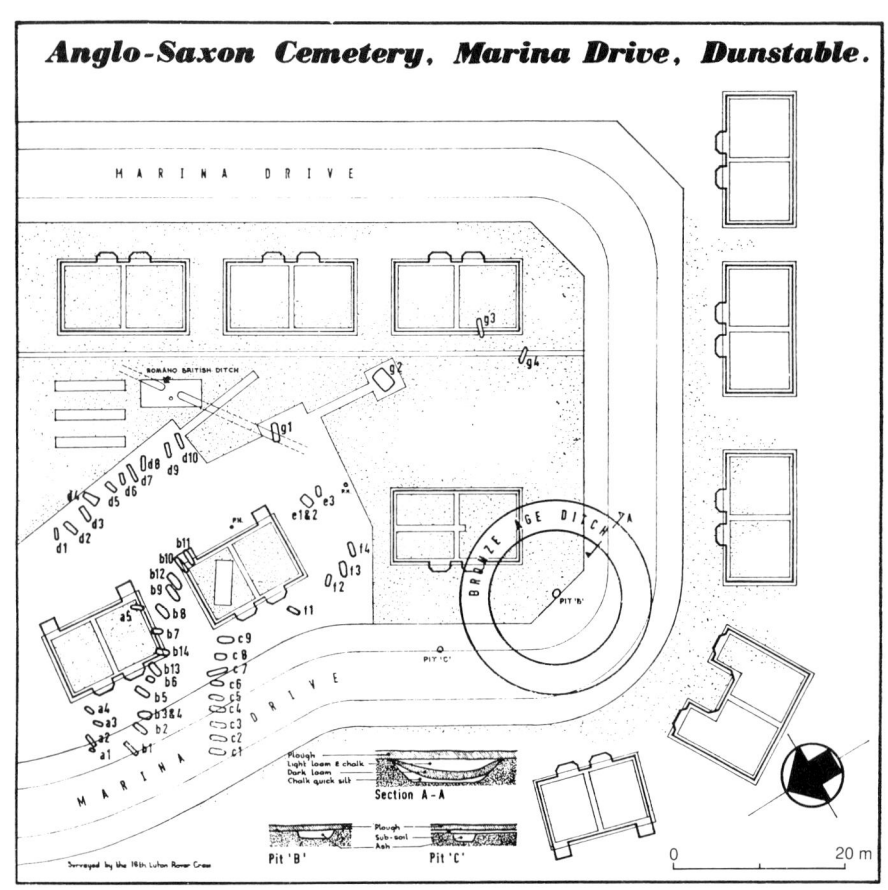

Fig. 50. Plan of Saxon Cemetery, Marina Drive, Dunstable.

The Saxon Cemetery at Marina Drive, Dunstable

In August 1957 builders at work on a new housing estate unearthed a skull and a spearhead on the hitherto open downland where Marina Drive now stands. The site was on the crest of the plateau which juts out from the spur of the Downs to the north-west of the town, about 1.5 km west of Watling Street and some three hundred metres north of the present line of the Icknield Way (Fig. 50).

The burial place of a small Saxon community was uncovered. The graves were grouped in a rough quarter circle around a Bronze Age barrow, where more than two thousand years earlier a cremation had taken place (see Chapter 3). The Saxons themselves sometimes erected barrows over important burials (as they probably did over the Puddlehill warrior). Graves were then sometimes grouped around these barrows, or around the burial mounds of earlier peoples, as here at Marina Drive.

The skeletons lay in shallow graves sunk 20–45 cm into the natural chalk and they were covered by only 15 cm of top soil. In all, forty-nine graves were identified although not all of them could be excavated.

One remarkable feature is the age distribution of the dead. This is quite unlike that of the few Saxon cemeteries for which comparable figures exist. Briefly, only one person in ten lived beyond the age of forty, and of those that did, three were women. On the other hand, sixteen young men were buried as against only three young women and, of the children, the evidence suggests that fully half were boys between the ages of twelve and fifteen. This means that either the community was sadly short of wives or that men died five times as easily as women. Over half the dead were men and boys of an age to fight and at least three had been wounded to the bone before death. It seems likely that many of them fell while defending their settlement. Men died young in Saxon England, but the apparent absence of anyone over the age of forty-five suggests that the community was not established very long. From the ages of the dead the inference is that it probably existed for some twenty years.

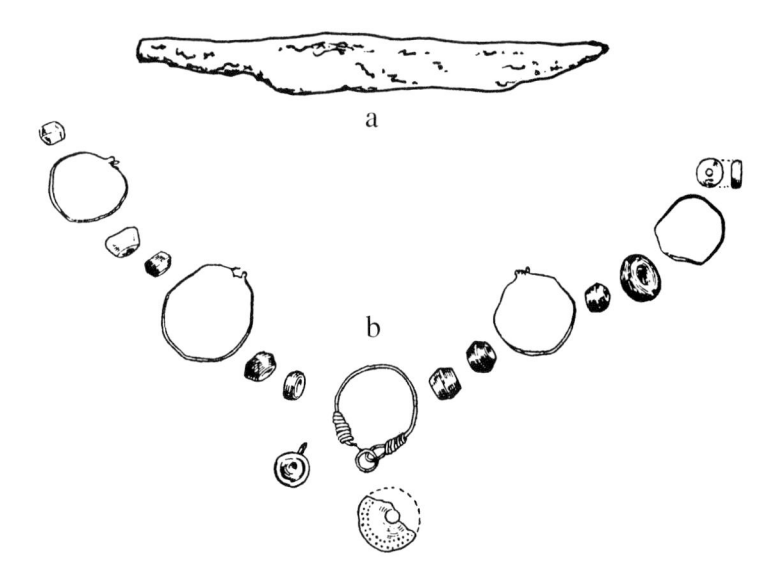

Fig. 51. Grave Goods from the Marina Drive Cemetery (Scale 1:2). *a*, Iron knife, one of many found with the burials; *b*, Dress festoon made up of silver wire rings, glass beads and two pendants, one of bronze and one of silver.

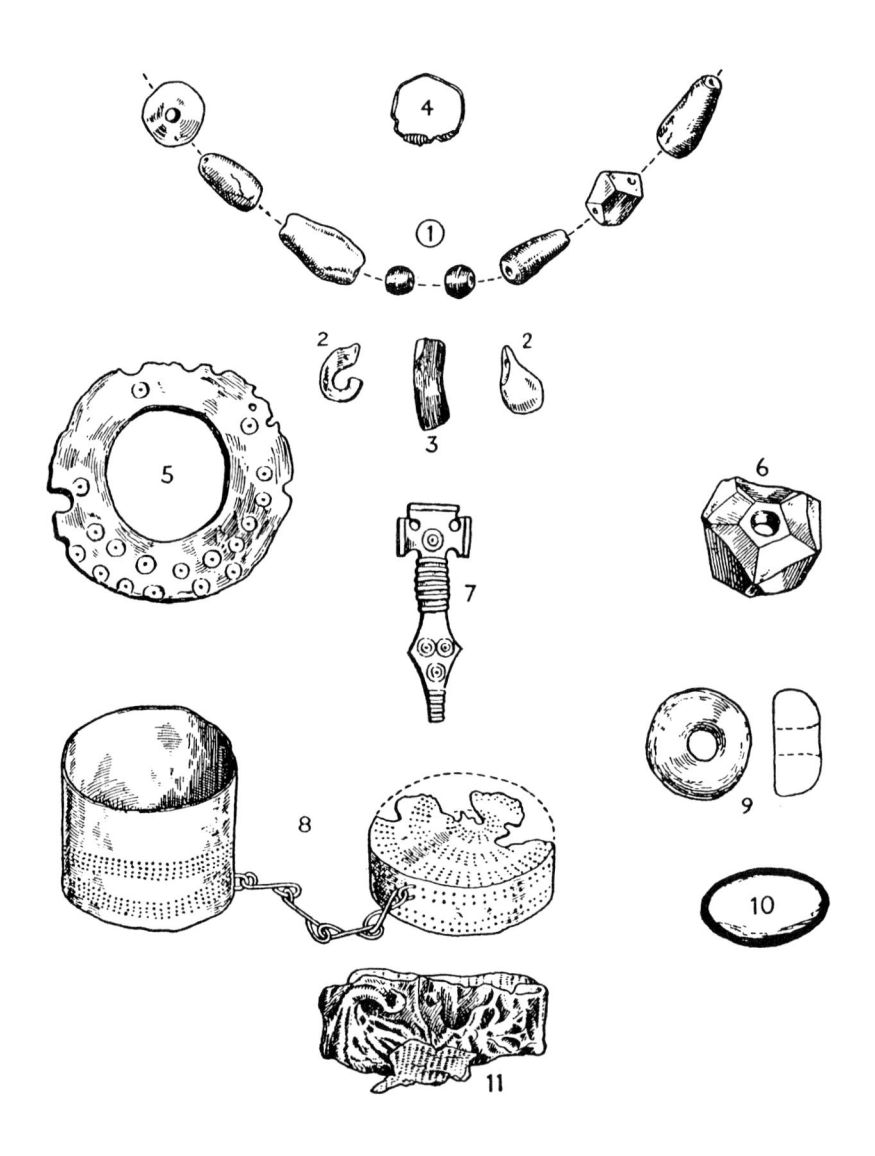

Fig. 52. Grave Goods from the Marina Drive Cemetery (Scale 1:2).

112

The adults of this community were tall: the average height of the men was 5 ft 9 $^1/_2$ ins (177 cm), with one man 6 ft 1 in (186 cm), and of the women 5 ft 3 $^1/_2$ ins (161 cm). This is taller than both the average for Dunstable's Romano-British cemetery and the modern average, but of course the Marina Drive sample is small (13 men and 4 women).

Their teeth were in very good condition even for Saxons, whose dental health was usually good.

The pattern of early death is heightened by the unusual affection lavished on the graves of the children (reminding us of the Dunstable Roman cemetery). Nearly all the men and half the women were buried with nothing but the clothes that they were wearing when they died. Four of the younger children, however, were buried with a wealth far greater than that of their elders and the graves of ten of the eighteen children contained at least a small bead or some other token. Some had amulets or good luck charms: there were two beaver teeth, for instance, drilled to take a small bronze ring. (The beaver was still a native British species at this time.) In three graves there were cowrie shells (as in one of the Puddlehill houses). Two of the men were buried with small pouches of human teeth (not their own) which must have had some magical or lucky significance.

They also placed household articles in the graves. What had once been a purse survived as a smudge of leather stain on the chalk below the rusted iron of the clip. There were two small bronze work boxes in which Saxon housewives had kept wool and flax thread. A silver locket decorated with a punch pattern of triangles and lozenges formed part of one of the richest necklaces. In one joint grave were found a bone comb, a pair of shears and an iron chain with a hook at one end and a shackle at the other. This was later identified as part of a pair of rudimentary scales. One small child had been buried with a bronze girdle-hanger – a device which would be fastened to the belt and from which workboxes and other small articles would hang.

Further items included a sharpening steel, spindle whorls, a hanging-bowl escutcheon and a variety of iron knives. Fragments of Roman glass – probably chance finds – had been treasured as ornaments. Few weapons

1	Festoon of beads. Amethyst, glass, amber and fishbone
2	Pendants of fishbone
3	Pendant of beaver tooth
4	Silver wire ear-ring
5	Bone ring
6	Faceted crystal
7	Silvered bronze brooch
8	Bronze workbox
9	Stone spindle whorl
10	Polished milky quartz pebble
11	Bronze mount with fragment of material

were found. The Argyll Avenue cemetery at Luton is typical of the long-established Saxon cemeteries throughout lowland Britain. It produced sixteen spears, one sword, eight shield bosses and thirty-two brooches. At Marina Drive on the other hand were found only one spear, two sword-knives (called scramasaxes) and no shield bosses.

We do not know where the Saxons who were buried at Marina Drive actually lived – though one small clue has survived. In the grave of an eight-year-old child a cake of puddled chalk at the feet still retained the imprint of the woven pattern of a shoe or sock. This suggests that their dwellings were on the upland chalk rather than in the valley of Totternhoe, or at least that the child died there.

Early Christian Cemeteries

If we compare the jewellery and personal items found in several of the Marina Drive graves with those of the woman on Puddlehill, the difference in style and fashion is very apparent (Plate 21 and Fig. 52). Only one brooch was found at Marina Drive and it seems to have been an heirloom: a very early type which had lost its pin and had probably been sewn to the sleeve of one of the children. There are few of the coloured inlaid beads of opaque glass. Instead there are beads of plain, coloured glass, amethyst, amber and fish-bone, and little bronze pendants called bracteates, all these often linked in a festoon by rings of silver wire, which was also used for single ear-rings.

This is the Kentish fashion, whereas the Puddlehill jewellery was West Saxon.

The Marina Drive cemetery is one of a new type, dating to the second half of the seventh century and found widely distributed in England as far north as Yorkshire. These cemeteries have many common characteristics: they are in new burial grounds; a high proportion of the graves, which are usually laid out in rows, contain nothing but the skeleton, or perhaps just a knife with the bones; the jewellery and other objects show a strong Kentish influence.

There was another cemetery of this type near Leighton Buzzard at Chamberlains Barn (II).

When the original report on the Marina Drive cemetery was published it was believed that these cemeteries belonged to communities originating in Kent, but further study has led to the belief that they are the earliest Christian Saxon cemeteries. Saint Augustine landed in Kent in 597 and the conversion of that kingdom followed. From there Christianity spread, with setbacks and at varying speeds. Mercia, in which Bedfordshire and Buckinghamshire lay at that time, became officially Christian in the second half of the seventh century, the period of the Marina Drive cemetery. The original Saxon church at Wing, near Leighton Buzzard, dates from the 660s.

The coming of Christianity would account for several features of these cemeteries: they were established on new sites to dissociate them from the pagan religion; a large proportion of the burials was made without grave-offerings, which were frowned on by the church, though the practice of burying personal possessions with the dead was difficult to stamp out and in fact continued for some time. When considering the objects from such a burial ground we should remember that an absence of finds may indicate not poverty but piety.

The Kentish style of jewellery, which had in fact come to Kent from the Continent, may have been adopted as a new fashion associated with the new religion, rather as "ethnic" dress became fashionable in the 1960s along with Eastern forms of meditation.

The finds from the Marina Drive excavation, as well as those from Puddlehill, Chamberlains Barn and the Luton Saxon burials can be seen in Luton Museum, where they make an impressive display.

The Mystery of the Five Knolls

The Bronze Age burials in the Five Knolls have already been discussed, but one of these barrows concealed some grim relics of Saxon times. In 1929 G. C. Dunning and R. E. M. (afterwards Sir Mortimer) Wheeler excavated nearly one hundred skeletons from around Barrow 5. There were ten groups of young adults, most of whom were male; six of the groups had been laid in orderly rows, one batch often displacing the skulls and limbs of the burials beneath them. Near the surface of the site but not in the graves themselves lay a variety of finds, ranging from an Iron Age brooch to a Roman goblet, sixth century Saxon pottery and a late Saxon buckle. One skeleton had a pierced Roman coin at his neck. Otherwise there was nothing: no brooches, necklaces or weapons which one would normally expect in an early Anglo-Saxon cemetery. More skeletons were found buried sporadically around the mass burial, some cutting through earlier graves. In many cases their wrists were crossed behind their backs as if they had been lashed together.

Who were they and who killed them? This is a fascinating archaeological puzzle to which no positive answer can yet be given. The excavators originally suggested that the mass burial had taken place at one time and that they were Saxon raiders who had been captured and slaughtered by the Romano-British. A counter suggestion was also made that they were Britons who had been massacred by the Saxons.

A third possibility was noted by Sir Mortimer Wheeler and has been developed by Dr. John Morris and others. The Five Knolls dominate the surrounding countryside and the Icknield Way. It would have been an ideal site for the meeting place of the local "folk-moot" (a kind of popular assembly) before the Manshead Hundred was established with its centre at Tingrith some time in the ninth or tenth century. One of the functions of such an assembly was the enforcement of justice and one of the instruments at its disposal was the gallows. Hanging, which involved slow strangulation rather than a broken neck, was the commonest Germanic form of execution. Anglo-Saxon society rested on two foundations: a mans's duty to his lord which was binding unto death, and the kinsman's duty to avenge any wrong done to one of his family. This vengeance could take the form of a strictly controlled vendetta or by the payment of money compensation – "wergild" – for the wrong done. Certain crimes, however, were "bootless" – that is, no compensation could be offered to atone for them. They included wilful (as opposed to accidental) homicide, arson, housebreaking, open theft and, above all, treachery to one's lord.

A number of execution cemeteries of the tenth and eleventh centuries have been identified, mainly in Wessex. If the Five Knolls was in fact the site of a gallows this would certainly explain the isolated haphazard burials on the surface of the barrow. The absence of personal ornaments, the lack of weapons and brooches, and the bound hands also become logical. It might possibly explain the mass burial if one assumes that these skeletons were not in fact all buried at the same time. It may be, therefore, that the Five Knolls was the focal centre of the district and the seat of justice and local government in the late Saxon period. The earlier objects found with the burials (sixth century pottery, a bronze tube, the pierced coin) could be relics from graves of the pagan Saxon period which had been disturbed by the later burials on the site and robbed of most surviving grave-goods.

A Changing Pattern

For nearly 3,000 years people lived, on and off, on Puddlehill; but now it has been unoccupied for thirteen hundred years. By the end of the seventh century the Saxon farmers had left their ruggedly-built home on the slope of the hill. Did they move into what is now Houghton Regis? The name Houghton (Old English *hoh tun*) means "settlement on the spur of a hill", a name which suits the situation of the Saxon farm much better than it does the more sheltered position of the modern village. Perhaps those early inhabitants brought the name down with them from the hill.

We have seen how the homes of these early Englishmen and women were scattered over the landscape This is quite usual at this period, when there is little evidence for what we sometimes think of as the "typical" English nucleated village, homes huddled together along a street or round a green.

During the seventh and eighth centuries the character of settlement in England seems to have changed. Up till then some of the Saxons seem to have lived on marginal land (like Puddlehill) perhaps unable to take over the better land because the British were still in possession. By the Mid-Saxon period the English were finally in a dominant position; and besides, the two peoples may already have become to some extent integrated. This made possible a relocation of settlements, sometimes called the "Mid-Saxon Shuffle", on to the most desirable sites, many of them still occupied as towns and villages today.

A move by the Marina Drive community down the hill to Totternhoe may account for the short period of use of their hillside cemetery. Perhaps from the eighth century onwards they were burying their dead where the churchyard still lies today, just over the way from the Roman villa. In recent years increasing evidence has been found in other parts of the country for estates and boundaries continuing with little change through the centuries of the Iron Age, the Roman Empire and the English settlements. Perhaps, then, it is not altogether fanciful to imagine the Totternhoe villa estate persisting as a British village through the post-Roman centuries until the natives were joined and dominated by the English newcomers.

So the pattern of our modern countryside with its clustered villages, each centred on the parish church, was first laid down when our English and British ancestors at last, after centuries of fighting, found a way to live together.

Museums

Dunstable
At the time of writing Dunstable has unfortunately no museum of its own, but the Dunstable Museum Trust has arranged, with the kind co-operation of the County Library and of Luton Museum, an interesting display in the Dunstable Library, Vernon Place. This contains many archaeological finds from the area, including some described in this book.

Luton
The greater part of the archaeological material from South Bedfordshire is housed in Luton Museum, Wardown Park. There is a fine display, which includes a section on Worthington Smith and his Palaeolithic discoveries, finds from the Five Knolls, from Puddlehill, and from the Anglo-Saxon cemeteries at Argyll Avenue, Marina Drive and Chamberlains Barn.

Bedford
This museum also has a good archaeological section, mainly covering the northern part of the county.

St. Albans
The Verulamium Museum in the village of St. Michaels houses the large quantity of very interesting material from the Roman city.

The Chiltern Open Air Museum
This is at Newland Park, Chalfont St. Giles. A reconstructed Iron Age house, based on the plan of one found on Puddlehill, is among the buildings re-erected there.

Book List

This list cannot be comprehensive. An attempt has been made to include references to the original reports of local excavations, as these are sometimes difficult to find. Also included are other works dealing specifically with our own area, and authorities cited in the text, such as Caesar and Bede. Apart from this, works on particular topics or periods are listed where they give a fuller account of subjects dealt with briefly in this book.

For readers seeking more general information there are many good books on archaeology, prehistory and the Roman period, and new ones are being written every year. The local library should have a selection. Check the year of publication: in some branches of the subject information and ideas soon become out of date.

Periodicals

These provide the latest news of discoveries and opinions.

Current Archaeology is a lively, well-illustrated and informative journal, read by both professionals and people with a general interest in the subject. It appears six times a year and is obtainable by post from 9 Nassington Road, London, NW3 2TX.

Bedfordshire Archaeology (formerly called the *Bedfordshire Archaeological Journal*) contains reports on sites in the county. It is obtainable from the Sales Officer, Alan Crawley, 305 Goldington Road, Bedford.

South Midlands Archaeology is published annually by Group 9 of the Council for British Archaeology and it contains archaeological reports from the counties of Bedford, Buckingham, Northampton and Oxford. It can be obtained from the Editor, Andrew Pike, Buckinghamshire County Museum, Church Street, Aylesbury.

The Manshead Journal reports on the work carried out by the Manshead Archaeological Society of Dunstable. It is free to members, but copies may be purchased from the Hon. Secretary, Barry Horne, Beaumont, Church End, Edlesborough, Dunstable, Beds.

General Works

Longworth, Ian, and Cherry, John. *Archaeology in Britain since 1945* (1986). This is a good summary for the general reader of the state of British archaeological knowledge in the mid 1980s.

Shire Archaeology is an excellent series published by Shire Books at very reasonable prices. The books cover subjects such as flints, pottery and metalwork of various periods, stone circles, hillforts etc.

Local Sites

Parish Surveys: the Historical Landscape and Archaeology is a series published by Bedfordshire County Council. Hockliffe, Kensworth, Caddington and Chalgrave are among the villages so far covered.

Matthews, C. L. *Occupation Sites on a Chiltern Ridge* (British Archaeological Reports 29, 1976) includes a foreword and summary by Professor C. F. C. Hawkes and full reports on the prehistoric sites excavated by the Manshead Society near Dunstable between 1951 and 1975. Readers who want more detailed information than is contained in *Ancient Dunstable* should consult *Occupation Sites* in the library, as it is now out of print.

Smith, Worthington G. *Dunstable: its History and Surroundings* (1904, reprinted 1986). This contains a popular account of the author's local researches, but it should be remembered that some of his conclusions and assumptions are now out of date.

Smith, Worthington G. "Early Man" in the *Victoria County History of Bedfordshire* pp. 145–174.

Smith, Worthington G. *Man the Primeval Savage* (1894). This includes accounts of his Palaeolithic discoveries in North London and in Bedfordshire, and also of barrows on Dunstable Downs.

Dyer, James F. "Worthington G. Smith" in *Bedfordshire Historical Records Society* publication 57 (1978). An account of the life and work of the Dunstable archaeologist.

Books relating to particular periods

CHAPTER 1
Sampson, C. Garth. *Paleoecology and Archeology of an Acheulian Site at Caddington, England* (1978). This is the report of an American excavation in 1971, which sought to locate the Palaeolithic floors discovered by W. G. Smith. It contains a re-assessment of Smith's finds.

Smith, Worthington G. All the books listed under "Local Sites" are particularly relevant to this period.

CHAPTER 2
Matthews, C. L. and Smith I. F. "New Neolithic Sites in Dorset and Bedfordshire" in the *Proceedings of the Prehistoric Society* (1964). Also the relevant sections of *Occupation Sites on a Chiltern Ridge*.

Smith, Worthington G. *Proceedings of the Society of Antiquaries*, 2nd series, 27 (1914–15) p. 143. This reports the Neolithic ditches observed at Maiden Bower.

CHAPTER 3
Dunning, G. C., and Wheeler, R. E. M. Report on the excavation of Barrow 5, Five Knolls in *Archaeological Journal* 88 (1931) p. 193.

Dyer, James F. "Barrows of the Chilterns" in *Archaeological Journal (1961)*.

Hawkes, C. F. C. "A Site of Late Bronze Age – Early Iron Age Transition at Totternhoe, Beds." in *Antiquaries Journal* 20 (1940) pp. 487–91.

Matthews, C. L., as listed under "Local Sites".

CHAPTER 4 and CHAPTER 5
Cotton, M. A., and Frere, S. S. "Ivinghoe Beacon Excavations 1963–65" in *Records of Buckinghamshire* Vol. 18, Part 3 (1968).

Cunliffe, Barry. *Iron Age Communities in Britain* (second edition 1978). A standard work on the period.

Dyer, James F. *Hillforts of England and Wales* (Shire Books 1981). This includes notes on Maiden Bower, Ravensburgh and other local sites.

Harding, D. W. *Hillforts* (1976). As well as a general discussion of hillforts, this contains excavation reports, including one by J. F. Dyer on Ravensburgh.

Livy. *History of Rome* (Penguin Books).

Matthews, C. L., as listed under "Local Sites".

Reynolds, Peter J. *Iron Age Farm, the Butser Experiment* (1979).

Saunders, C. "The Pre-Belgic Iron Age in the Central and Western Chilterns" in *Archaeological Journal* (1972). This includes a consideration of pottery from Puddlehill.

Smith, W. G. The paper listed under Chapter 2 includes a description of Maiden Bower and his excavation there.

CHAPTER 6
Branigan, Keith. *The Catuvellauni* (1985). This discusses what is known of the tribe and its territory, mainly during the Roman period.

Caesar, Julius. *The Conquest of Gaul* (Penguin Books).

Matthews, C. L., as listed under "Local Sites".

Wheeler, R. M. and T. V. *Verulamium: a Belgic and Two Roman Cities* (1936).

CHAPTER 7
Frere, Sheppard. *Britannia*. This is a standard work on Roman Britain first published in 1967, but since revised.

Frere, Sheppard. *Verulamium Excavations*. Vol. 1 (1972) reports the excavations of a row of shops along Watling Street, destroyed in Boudica's revolt.

Mann, J. C., and Penman, R. G. *Literary Sources for Roman Britain* (Lactor 11, 1977). A collection of all the quotations from classical Greek and Roman authors which mention Britain.

Matthews, C. L., and Hutchings, J. B. "A Roman Well at Dunstable" in *Bedfordshire Archaeological Journal* 7 (1972).

Matthews, C. L., and others. "A Romano-British Inhumation Cemetery at Dunstable" in *Bedfordshire Archaeological Journal* 15 (1981).

Matthews, C. L. "Bidwell Roman Site" in *South Midlands Archaeology* 16 (1986).

Roucoux, Omer. *The Roman Watling Street* (Dunstable Museum Trust 1984). Collects together the documentary evidence and includes illustrations.

Salway, Peter. *Roman Britain* (1981). The most recent comprehensive work on the subject.

Simco, Angela. *Survey of Bedfordshire – The Roman Period* (1984). Well-illustrated account of all that is known about Roman Bedfordshire.

Smith, W. G. The paper listed under Chapter 2 contains an account of Roman finds in and near Maiden Bower.

Tacitus. *On Britain and Germany* (Penguin Books). This includes the biography of Tacitus' father-in-law Agricola, who had been Governor of Britain.

Wheeler, R. M. and T. V., as listed under Chapter 6.

CHAPTER 8
Anglo-Saxon Chronicle. Various editions.

Austin, W. "A Saxon Cemetery at Luton" in *Antiquaries Journal* 8 (1928). This is the report of finds from Argyll Avenue made during building and road-making.

Bede. *History of the English Church* (Penguin Books).

Davis, K. Rutherford. *Britons and Saxons The Chiltern Region 400–700* (1982).

Dunning, G. C., and Wheeler, R. E. M., as listed under Chapter 3. This includes a report of the Saxon mass burial at Five Knolls.

Gildas. *The Ruin of Britain* (Phillimore 1978).

Hyslop, Miranda. "Two Anglo-Saxon Cemeteries at Chamberlains Barn, Leighton Buzzard" in *Archaeological Journal* 120 (1963) pp. 161–200.

Matthews, C. L., "The Anglo-Saxon Cemetery at Marina Drive" and "Saxon remains on Puddlehill" in *Bedfordshire Archaeological Journal* 1 (1962).

Matthews, C. L., and Hawkes, Sonia Chadwick. "Early Saxon Settlements and Burials on Puddlehill" in *Anglo-Saxon Studies in Archaeology and History* 4 (1985).

Morris, John. *The Age of Arthur.* A comprehensive, stimulating and controversial study of "the Dark Ages" by an old friend of Dunstable archaeologists.

Wilson, D. M. *The Archaeology of Anglo-Saxon England* (1976).

Acknowledgments

A number of the acknowledgments made by C. L. Matthews in the original edition of this book should be repeated here: to the late Mr. C. E. Stevens and the late Dr. John Morris for reading the text and making helpful suggestions; to Mr. E. C. Hawes (for many years Secretary of the Manshead Society) for help with Chapter 1; to Mr. John Payne for advice on Chapters 2 and 3 and to Mr. R. Wayman for help with Chapter 8.

In addition to these the co-author of this revised version would like to express grateful thanks to Mrs. Sonia Hawkes for very kindly reading Chapter 8 and making helpful comments on it. Dr. Robin Holgate of Luton Museum, as well as giving much assistance in locating references and providing space to draw items from the museum's collection, was kind enough to read through Chapters 1 to 6 and gave much useful advice (including the modification of androcentric language!) Dr. Peter Reynolds gave us the benefit of his unrivalled knowledge and experience of Iron Age farming and building.

Some plans and drawings have been retained from the first edition: the plan of Marina Drive surveyed by the 16th Luton Rover Crew and the illustrations of finds from the Marina Drive cemetery by the late Mr. Alec Fowler, and some pottery drawings by the late Mrs. Dorothy Fowler. Of the new illustrations, the plans in Figs. 15, 18, 46 and 47 and most of the objects in Figs. 17, 19, 23, 24, 25, 28, 31 and 34 were drawn by Mr. John Bailey and we are grateful for his permission to use them. The plans Fig. 1 and Fig. 32 have been specially prepared and drawn by Mr. John Hitchcock. Many of the other illustrations were also drawn specifically for this book. The art work for the cover, based on the skeleton of the Saxon Warrior from Puddlehill, was carried out by Mr. John Gillbe, to whom we are also grateful.

Several members of the Society, including our present Site Director Mr. Dave Warren, made useful suggestions during the preparation of the final text, and the writer is particularly grateful to Mr. John Hitchcock for his sharp eye and logical mind, which removed many woolly sentences and inconsistencies in orthography. Any which remain, together with all other errors, are the responsibility of the writer. Mr. Barry Horne has worked extremely hard and efficiently in organising the whole project and in preparing the book to go to the printer laid out in its final form. Thanks are due to Derek Sheills for assistance with the typesetting.

Sheila Freeman has arranged the finances. Special thanks are due to those members who agreed to lend money to finance this publication.

The production of this book is only possible because it was preceded by years of excavation and of study of the finds. For this work we are grateful to all our members, past and present, to experts in various fields who have helped us with information and advice, and also of course to the landowners who permitted our activities. C. L. Matthews expressed thanks to the Tunnel Cement Co., the Rugby Portland Cement Co. and the Associated Portland Cement Co., and also to Mr. George Pratt, Mr. P. A. Hemmings and Mr. John Batchelar. To these names we must now add above all that of Mr. J. B. Stevens, who made us welcome for so many years on the Friary Field, and also of Mr. Flory, for freedom to work on the field next to it. The Hallsworth Trust kindly permitted excavation on their land at Bidwell.

Our work over the years has been made much easier by assistance from the Dunstable Borough Council and their successors the South Bedfordshire District Council, who not only found us headquarters where we can store materials and carry out post-excavation work, but also assisted financially to make possible the rescue excavation of Roman Dunstable before redevelopment took place.